Military Service
in the *Abbott*
Family

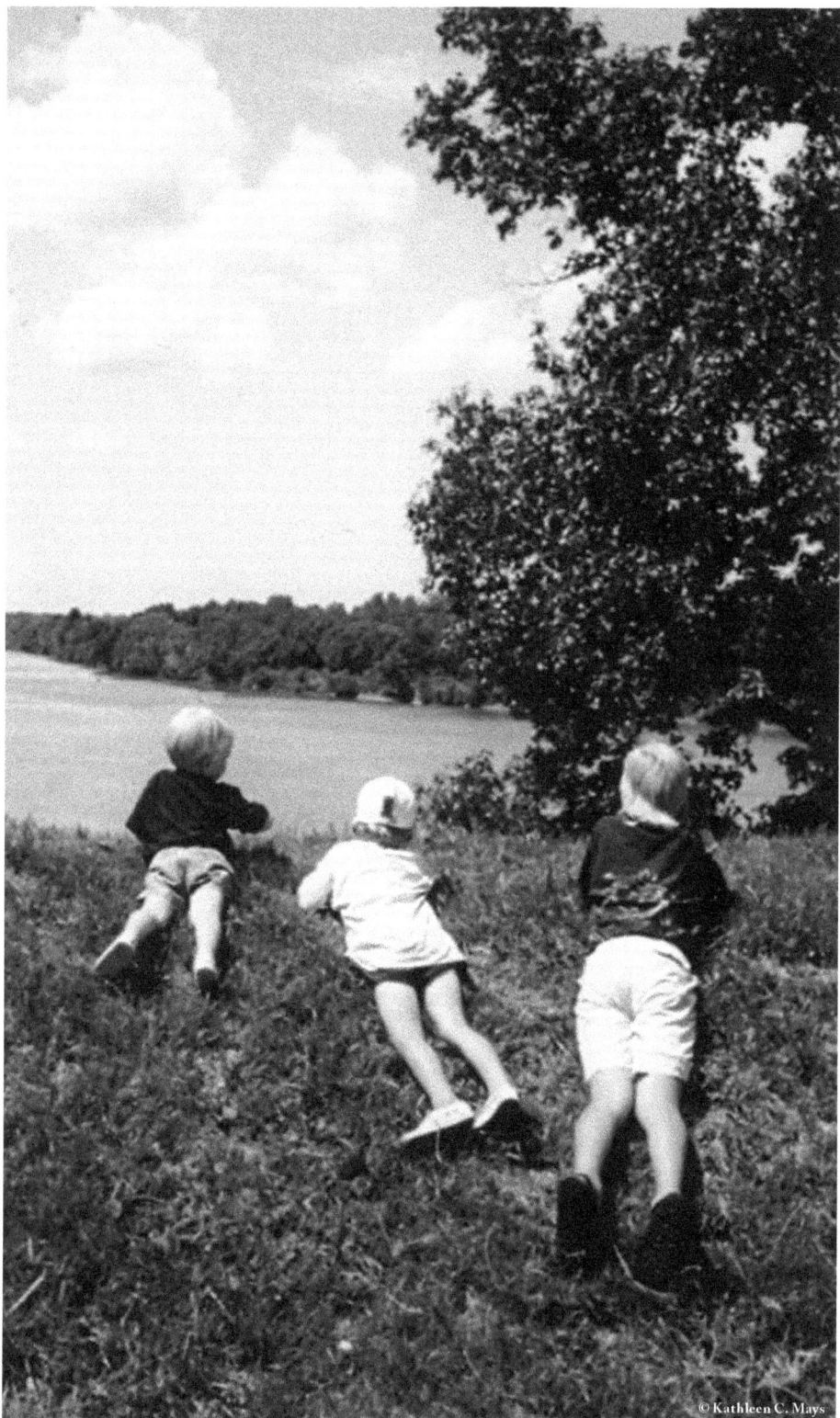

Military Service

in the

Abbott

Family

with Historical Highlights of the USS Midway

JRemington

JRP

PRESS™

JRemington Press
1050 East 3300 South, Suite 204
Salt Lake City, Utah 84109
(801) 975-0109
JRemingtonPress.com

ISBN: 979-8-9881063-1-9
Salt Lake City, Utah
First Printing, First Edition, July 2023

1 2 3 4 5 6 7 8 9 10

Artist and Designer, Austin J. Record

My Father

As he would hold out his big, rough hand,
My tiny fingers would clutch onto his,
And I would proudly walk with him.

I had many debates,
With friends of my youth,
Always declaring, insisting,
He was the strongest and most handsome man,
In the whole world.
He was and is.

Throughout my life,
I have had moments,
When no one could reach me,
Excepting my father.
Always firmly, respectfully, lovingly.

If I composed on paper,
All of his positive attributes,
It would take volumes,
To log them all.

I have unfailingly felt,
Unconditional love
From my dad.

For all that he's been to me,
I will never stop trying, aiming,
To be all that he wants me to be.

And when people call me,
a "daddy's girl",
I will beam with pride,
As he has always owned my heart

~ Kathleen Cary Mays

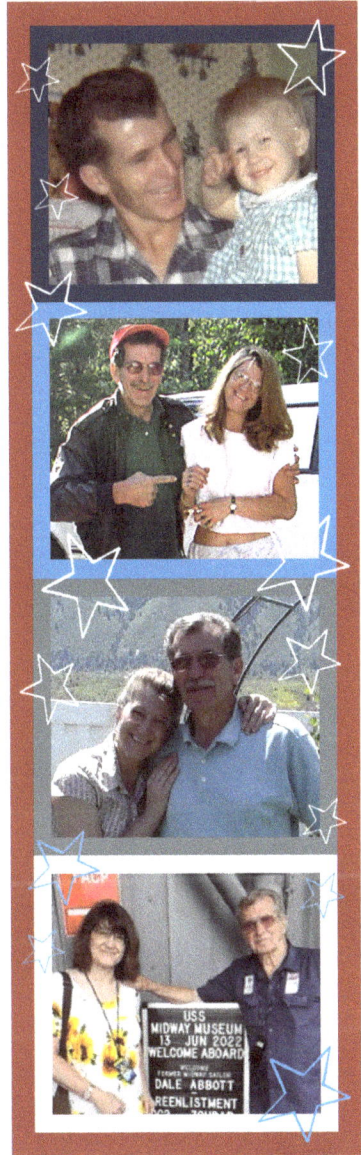

I dedicate this work to the man who has always been
a hero in my world, my dad, Dale Cary Abbott.

Table of Contents

Acknowledgements

The production of this book was a powerful experience for me. I would first like to thank my youngest son, Austin. His patience with me as I learned the ins and outs of preparing a book for publication was outstanding. His skills in the creative field have made this project into a work of art.

John, my husband, supports every new endeavor I begin. As my best friend, I bounce my ideas off him and he gives me honest input. I have told him that our two minds together would make a great dictionary. He knows definitions and I spell really well.

This book may not have come to fruition without the faith that my mentor, Kent Merrell, had in me. I'll not forget the day I excitedly showed him a list of the books I've been writing and heard him confidently say, "Kathleen, you're already an author!" His belief in me is treasured.

My parents, Dale and Louise Abbott, have shared so many stories which turned my interest into a passionate quest for more narratives. The stories of their grandparents, parents, and their own lives has enlivened these past individuals from simpler times. I'm proud of who I am and I owe the foundation of that to my two exceptional parents.

My three sons, Christopher, Nicholas, and Austin are driving forces that provide me many reasons to do good things in my life. I don't think you could possibly know how blessed I feel to be your mother. Each ancestral saga that I learn about becomes one more reason to document them for you to read, when you're ready.

I'm thankful that my sister, Teresa, is always so interested when I stumble upon genealogical stories and images. When I find a great picture or an interesting story, I want to share it with her, my lifelong cohort, as soon as I can. It is a heartwarming reminder that we have yet one more important connection.

When it comes to my uncles, Lawrence and Neal Abbott, it is "funderful" for me to learn more about these two men whom I have always looked up to. They've fed my passion for learning more about serving in the military by trusting me enough with their personal details and stories.

I'd like to mention my nieces and nephew, Ashley, Adriann, Aspen, and Wyatt (and of course their children). They may not realize it, but they too, give me another level of motivation. I want them to learn about those who came before them and be proud of the blood that courses through our veins.

I would specifically like to thank cousins Laurie Meredith and Danny Bringard for contributing information about their fathers. I hope I've done well by them. For all of my other cousins, I can guarantee that you have been thought about during this process. The support of our family members, seen or unseen, has been crucial.

Thank you to each family member who not only contributed facts but also provided a warm, human connection to our purpose. It's a privilege to have family relationships and to each of our kith and kin, this is for you!

Preface

Started in 2019, this project has been a labor of love; love of who we are, love of family, love of country, and love of what we believe in.

The primary motivation to create this anthology was our desire to make a unique and memorable birthday gift for Christopher Shawn Abbott, the son of Kathleen and the older brother of Austin. An unexpected sense of gratitude grew from that decision, becoming a gift unto ourselves. It became evident how many individuals and families sacrificed, whether they were drafted or enlisted. For that, I am inspired by them.

Each of the military heroes highlighted in this book are ancestors or close relatives of the children of Dale Cary and Janice Louise Philpott Abbott. We will note whether the veteran is in Dale's "Abbott / Cary line" or in Janice's "Philpott / Bringard line" on each individual's profile page.

Kathleen has compiled all research and text, beginning with documentation received years ago from both of her grandmothers, Trula Marie Cary Abbott and LaDonna Bringard Philpott Peck. Each of these beautiful women fostered Kathleen's love for genealogy and family history, lasting a lifetime.

Austin James Record has completed all document layout, and photo manipulation and/or restoration, with a desire to make this an ongoing gift of love for his brother and entire family.

It's been an enlightening and rewarding journey.

How This Book Came To Be

One interest my sister and I enjoyed as children, and consistently into adulthood, has been hearing the stories of our parents' lives before we were an 'us.' One part of this has been hearing about Dad's service in the U.S. Navy.

As a family, we enjoyed three different trips to San Diego, California to visit the USS Midway Museum. After the first two trips, I felt an undeniable urge to document my thoughts and feelings. The combined joy of experiencing the ship as a tangible backdrop to the scenarios of Dad's tales with my love of writing and my lifelong passion for family history, was a great recipe for motivation.

© Austin J. Record

The USS Midway received the Retention Excellence Award in 1986 and 1987 represented by the gold anchors.

I had such a fulfilling experience writing and choosing pics from my photographs for my idea of a blog post. When Austin and I decided to create a digital book for Christopher's birthday, I didn't need to look very far for inspiration.

The USS Midway Museum

Each time we visited the museum, I was impressed by the staff, both paid and volunteered. The system they incorporated, with paid staff's hat being one specific color and volunteer staff's hat being a different color, is helpful when assistance is needed.

The digital tour guides are simply awesome! Even the little ones enjoyed our visit. I wasn't surprised at how excited I felt to visit because my dad served in the G Division on the Midway from 1958 to 1961.

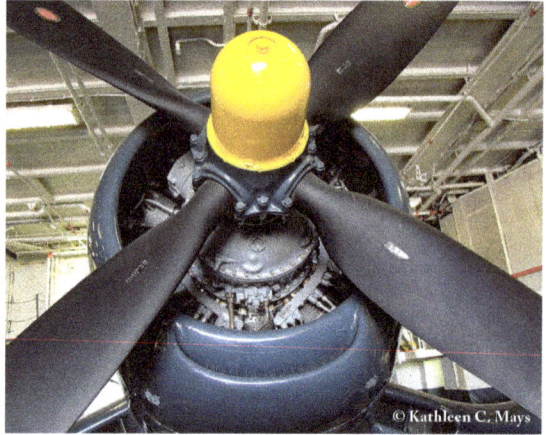
© Kathleen C. Mays

A huge benefit of visiting the ship with my father was having our own personal tour guide and hearing even more stories from him about his Navy service. What really warmed my heart was seeing the excitement on his face and hearing the enthusiasm in his voice as he communicated his memories to us.

© Kathleen C. Mays

Her Beginnings

There is a lot of fascinating history connected with this amazing ship! Before I share some of my research, which will simply skim over the huge amount of information that is available for Her, I'd like to define the four celebrated events in a ship's life; keel laying (laid down), launching, commissioning and decommissioning.

The USS Midway was laid down on October 27, 1943 by Newport News Shipbuilding Co. in Newport News, Virginia.

She was launched on March 20, 1945, being sponsored by Mrs. Bradford William Ripley, Jr., commissioned on September 10, 1945, eight days after Japan surrendered and decommissioned on April 11, 1992. Her stateside home ports were Norfolk, Virginia and Alameda, California.

A Battle Called Midway

She, our lady of the sea, was named after the significant Battle of Midway in June of 1942, only six months after Japan attacked Pearl Harbor. The Battle of Midway was a major naval battle in the Pacific Theater of World War II.

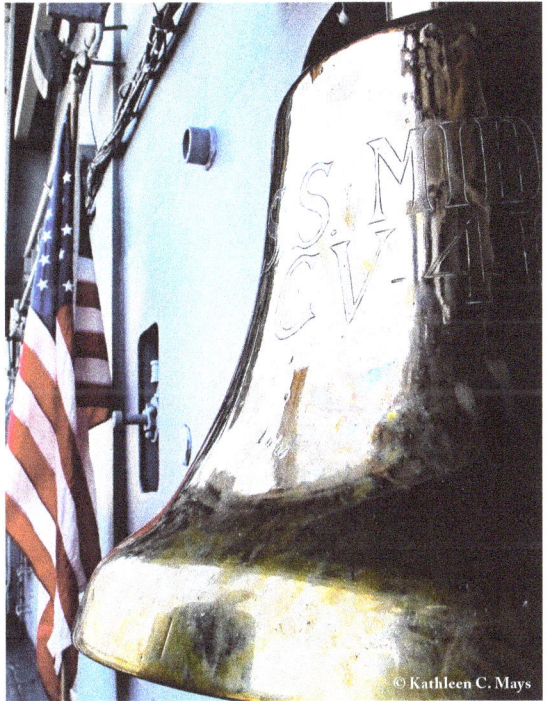
© Kathleen C. Mays

The U.S. Navy, under Admirals Chester W. Nimitz, Frank J. Fletcher, and Raymond A. Spruance, defeated an attacking fleet of the Imperial Japanese Navy north of Midway Atoll, inflicting devastating damage on the enemy. There is so much historical detail about this vessel that I am having some difficulty choosing what to highlight on.

Outstanding Films

There are several movies about this battle with one of the greatest being a documentary directed and produced by Rear

Place setting for the lost sailor.

Admiral John Ford, USNR, entitled "The Battle of Midway" featuring Henry Fonda as the narrator.

In fact, speaking of movies, an incident on Midway's deck on June 23, 1951 occurred and footage of the crash has been used in several films such as Men of the Fighting; Lady, Midway; and The Hunt for Red October.

As Commander George Chamberlain Duncan was attempting a landing, a downdraft aft of the stern caused him to crash. His plane's forward fuselage broke away, rolled down the deck and he suffered burns.

During decommissioning in 1992, the Midway, its sailors, and their families were filmed for the movie "At Sea", a documentary on carrier life which was shown only at the Navy Museum in Washington, D.C.

Her Seafaring Affairs

Some of the waters She sailed, although not in chronological order, were The Persian Gulf, The Pacific, The Labrador Sea and Davis Strait in The Northern Atlantic, The Caribbean, The Mediterranean, Arctic Waters, The Indian Ocean, around Cape Horn, and The Arabian Sea. She was much too large to go through the Panama Canal.

Notable Details

She had 40 commanding officers in her career with Captain Joseph F. Bolger being the first. The USS Midway was the longest-serving aircraft carrier in the 20th century. She was actually the third American ship to bear the name of Midway. The first USS Midway was a fleet auxiliary whose name was changed to the USS Panay in April of 1943. The second ship was a jeep carrier whose name was changed to the USS Saint Lo, which sank on October 25, 1944 as the result of a kamikaze attack.

After Midway's shakedown in the Caribbean, she joined the US Atlantic Fleet. A shakedown is a nautical term that is used pertaining to a ship's first cruise before she enters service or after major overhauls to simulate working conditions, test performance, and familiarize the crew with the new vessel.

Unusual Events In Her Career

In 1922, the Navy League of New York proposed an official observance day for appreciation of Naval service. They proposed the date of October 27th in honor of President Theodore Roosevelt's birth date. Just so you know, this is still a celebrated day but it was not on my calendar. I entered the date in my calendar and will celebrate every year in gratitude.

North Island, San Diego Bay, viewed from Cabrillo Monument.

As it is suggested to be the "grandest commemoration of all", on Navy Day in 1945, a seven-mile line of U.S. Navy warships anchored in the Hudson River and some 1,200 Navy planes flew overhead in commemoration of the event. This was the first Navy Day after World War II ended and it sounds spectacular!

Modernization

The Midway went through several different extensive modernization programs in her life. She also had three different designations, CV-41, CVB-41 and CVA-41. For those of

Stained glass in the Midway's chapel, ca. 2022.

us who have to look up the meaning of these codes, (yes, me) CV is Aircraft Carrier, CVB is Aircraft Carrier Large and CVA is Aircraft Carrier Attack.

Her Retirement

The Lady, Midway was decommissioned at Naval Air Station North Island on April 11, 1992 with Secretary of Defense Dick Cheney as the main speaker.

On September 30, 2003, Midway began her journey from the Navy Inactive Ship Maintenance Facility at Bremerton, Washington to San Diego, California in preparation for use as a museum and memorial.

Fantail Restaurant, ca. 2014.

She was docked in October at the Charles P. Howard Terminal in Oakland, California. The work on the Broadway Pier in San Diego was not finished and ready for her until January 10, 2004. She was moved and opened to the public on June 7, 2004 as a museum. In her first year of operation, she received 879,281 visitors which is double the expected attendance.

My Captivation

To digest my thoughts at this moment, I am in awe and almost overwhelmed with the information that is out there ready for us to read and learn from. They now have a research library on the USS Midway Museum. They have a restaurant

Image credit: Austin J. Record

Painting by Richard DeRosset on a wall of the USS Midway, ca. 2022.

for hungry guests and a wonderful gift shop with a variety of items and historical memorabilia. If anyone were to ask me if I would recommend going there for a visit, my answer would be an emphatic "H*** YES!"

Sources

1. USS Midway Wikipedia Article, https://en.m.wikipedia.org/wiki/USS_Midway_(CV-41), accessed 12 September 2018

2. Battle of Midway Wikipedia Article, https://en.m.wikipedia.org/wiki/Battle_of_Midway, accessed 27 January 2023

3. Midway Sailor, USS Midway CV-41, https://www.midwaysailor.com/midway/history.html, accessed 14 September, 2018

4. Collegiate Water Polo Association, https://collegiatewaterpolo.org/john-t-blackburn-united-states-naval-academy-alumnus-water-polo-athlete-aviator-double-ace-founding-commander-of-the-jolly-rogers/, accessed 28 January 2023

5. Midway Sailer, USS Midway Commanding Officers, https://www.midwaysailor.com/midway/commandoff.html. accessed 15 September 2018

6. Dale Cary Abbott, interviewed 11 September 2018

7. Military.com, https://www.military.com/navy-birthday/the-two-navy-holidays.html, accessed 13 September 2018

8. National Naval Naval History Aviation http://www.navalaviationmuseum.org/history-up-close/navy-day/, Aviat accessed 14 September 2018

9. NavSource Naval History, http://www.navsource.org/archives/02/41.htm, accessed 27 January 2023

10. Naval Heritage and History, https://www.history.navy.mil/our-collections/photography/us-navy-ships/aircraft-carriers.htm,l accessed 28 January 2023

Christopher Shawn Abbott

Private Second Class · United States Army
Served 2011-2012
Of the Abbott / Cary line & of the Philpott / Bringard line

Christopher Shawn Abbott was born on the 4th of March, 1981 to Steven Timothy and Kathleen Cary Abbott Griffin in Murray, Salt Lake Co., Utah.

He was raised in the Salt Lake Valley and from childhood, always excelled in strategic plotting and military planning. He spent a great many years researching the American Civil War.

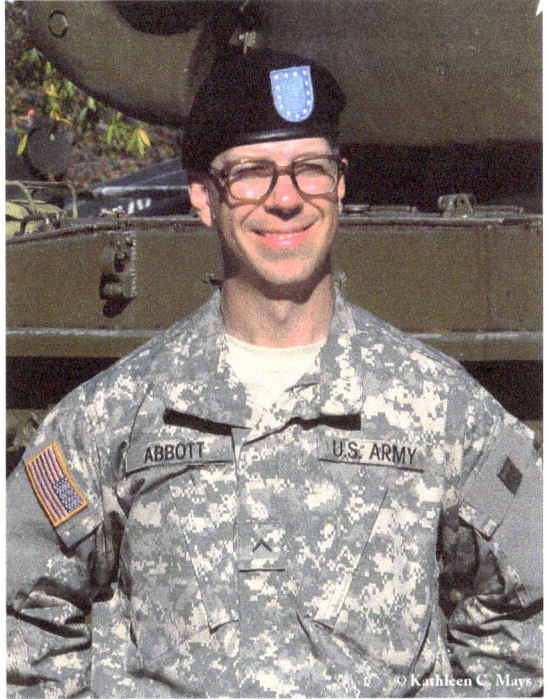

© Kathleen C. Mays

Christopher enlisted in the United States Army in Murray, Utah and entered Fort Jackson, South Carolina on the 9th of September 2011 for Basic Training.

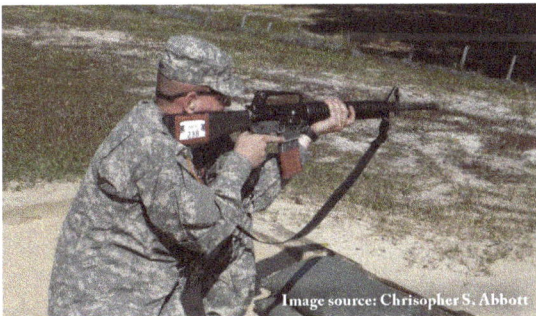

Image source: Chrisopher S. Abbott

He trained with the 2nd Platoon, Bravo Company, 2nd Battalion, 13th Infantry Regiment, 193rd Infantry Brigade. Their company motto was

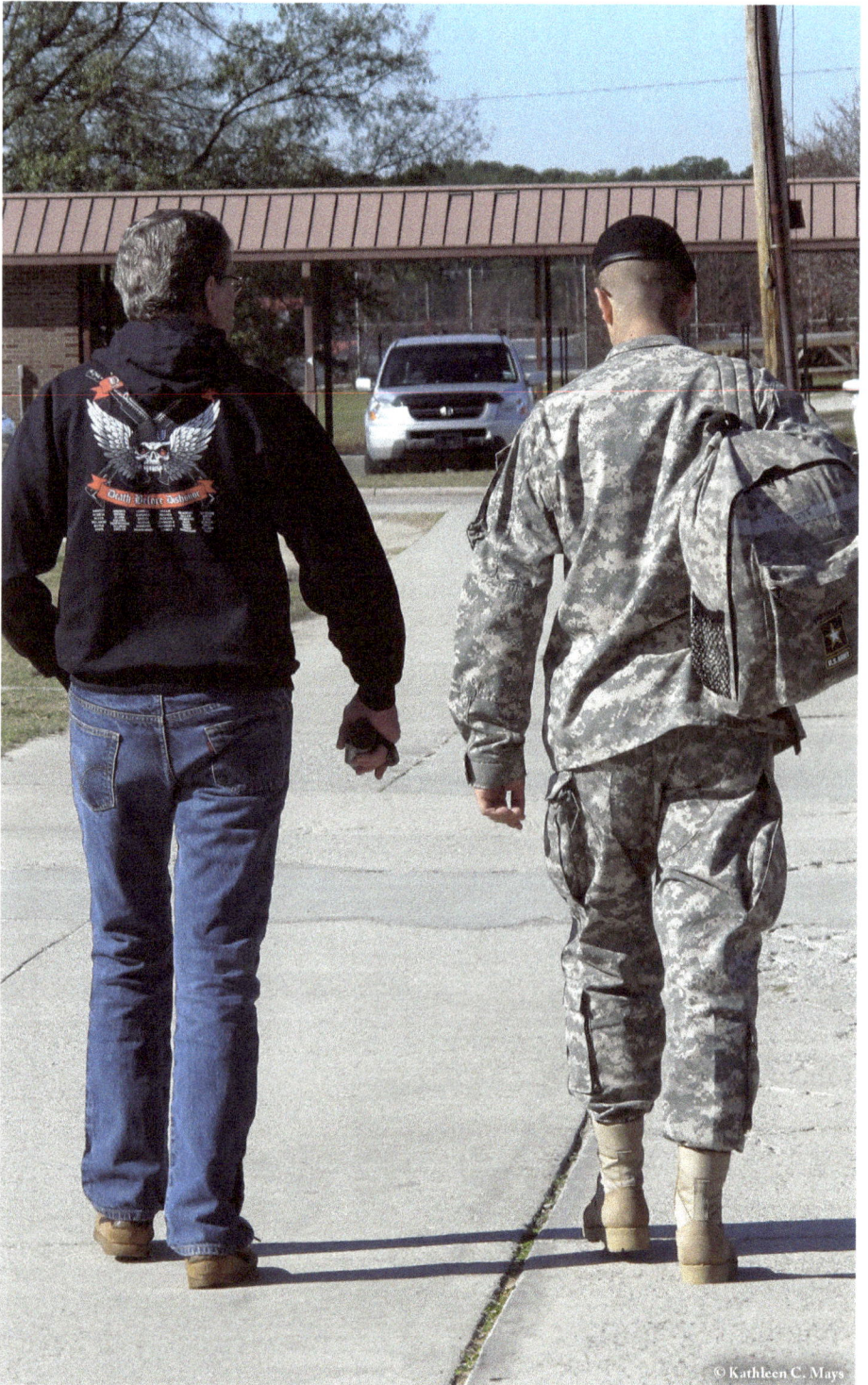

© Kathleen C. Mays

Grandfather and Grandson, Dale and Christopher Abbott, ca. 2011.

Military Service in the Abbott Family

"40 rounds", while their battalion motto was "First at Vicksburg".

He finished basic training in November 2011 and was then stationed at The Presidio of Monterey in California in the 4th Platoon, Alpha Company, 229th Military Intelligence Battalion. Here, their company motto was "Soldiers First" while their battalion motto was "Strength Through Intelligence".

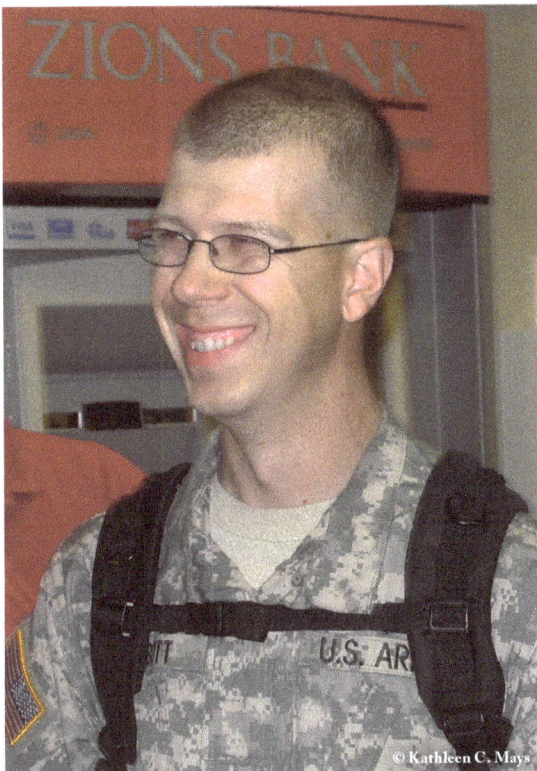

© Kathleen C. Mays

Image source: Chrisopher S. Abbott

He was proficient in his training as a Military Intelligence Analyst although an increasing medical issue developed in early 2012, which required an unplanned early discharge.

Information is included in this book with permission.

Sources:

11. Mays, Kathleen Cary Abbott, Personal Knowledge, documented 7 February 2019

Image source: Pixabay

12. Abbott, Alexis Ann Busath, "Details of Christopher Abbott's Military Service," Interview by Kathleen C. Mays, Military Service of the Abbotts, 20 February 2019

13. Abbott, Christopher Shawn, "Details of Christopher Abbott's Military Service," Interview by Kathleen C. Mays, Military Service of the Abbotts, 10 Mar 2019

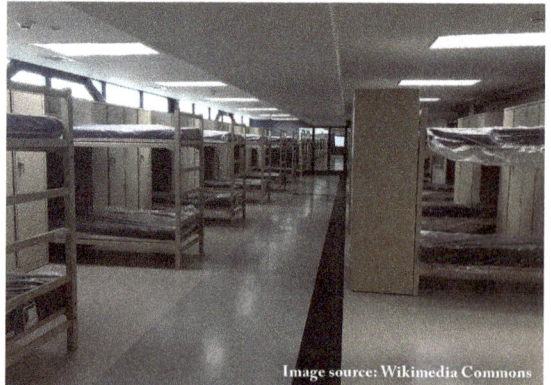
Image source: Wikimedia Commons

Fort Jackson, SC, Barracks

Neal Alan Abbott

Staff Sergeant E6 · United States Navy
United States Army Reserve · United States
National Guard Artillery · Served 1970-1988
Of the Abbott / Cary line

Neal Alan Abbott was born on the 27th of April, 1953 to Lawrence Elnathon and Trula Marie Cary Abbott in Delta, Millard Co., Utah. He was raised in the farming community of Sutherland, just a few miles outside of Delta.

Neal entered the United States Navy on the 28th of December, 1970. He reported to boot camp at San Diego, California, then attended Ship Fitter Class A School, also in San Diego.

Image source: Janice Louise Abbott

From left: Dale Shawn, Neal Alan, and Dale Cary Abbott, ca. 1972.

He received orders to the USS Samuel Gompers, AD-37, which was a Destroyer Tender, and they deployed to the Western Pacific, WestPac cruise two times.

During the two cruises, Neal and his Samuel Gompers shipmates visited Yokosuka, Japan, Subic Bay Phillipines, Hong Kong, Kaohsuing Republic of China, Taiwan (previously known as Formosa), and Danang Vietnam.

Image source: Wikipedia Commons

USS Samuel Gompers, ca. 1968.

Neal ranked as a Petty Officer 3rd Class during his active service in the Navy as a Hull Technician (fireman), performing tasks of damage control, piping and hull repair and maintenance while aboard the ship.

Some interesting details about the USS Samuel Gompers Class Destroyer Tender: She was laid down on the 9th of July, 1964, at Puget Sound Naval Shipyard, Bremerton, WA.

© Kathleen C. Mays

The Samuel Gompers launched on the 14th of May, 1966 and was commissioned as the USS Samuel Gompers (AD-37) on the 1st of July, 1967.

During the Vietnam War, USS Samuel Gompers participated in the campaign Vietnam Ceasefire, from the 9th to the 16th and from the 22nd to the 30th of April, 1972, earning her a campaign star for Vietnam War service.

She was decommissioned on the 27th of October, 1995, at Newport News Shipbuilding in Newport News, VA. and laid up at the Naval Inactive Ship Maintenance Facility in Portsmouth, VA.

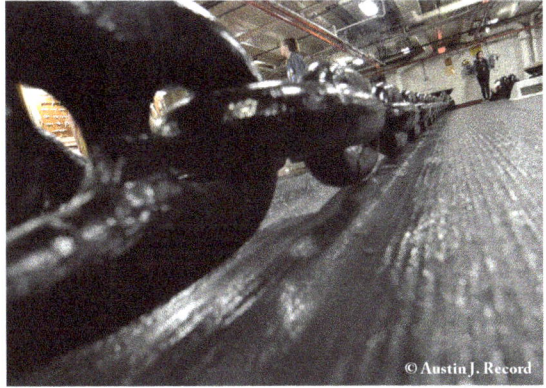
© Austin J. Record

AD-37, the 643 foot Tender / Repair Ship, moved to the National Defense Reserve Fleet, James River Group, Lee Hall, Virginia in November 1995, and struck from the Naval Register, 7 April 1999.

Her custody transferred to the Maritime Administration, for disposal on the 7th of April, 1999 followed with her Final Disposition. She was disposed of as a target on the 21st of July, 2003 in the VACAPES OPAREA, the Virginia Capes Operating Area off the coast of Virginia during fleet exercises.

Petty Officer Abbott was discharged in San Diego, California on the 10th of November, 1974 and later joined

Image source: Neal Abbott

The Army Reserve, 419th Transportation Company in Salt Lake City, Utah.

Following that he was a member of The Army National Guard 2nd Battalion 222nd Field Artillery in Fillmore, Utah and The 1457th Engineer Battalion out of Nephi, Utah, attaining the rank of E6 Staff Sergeant.

Information is included in this book with permission.

Sources

14.   Abbott, Neal Alan, "Details of Neal Abbott's Military Service," Interview by Kathleen Mays, Military Service of the Abbotts, 10 February 2019

15.   Navy: Together We Served, No Stronger Bond, USS Samuel Gompers (AD 37) Tender / Repair Ship, https://navy.togetherweserved.com/usn/servlet/tws.webapp.WebApp?cmd=UnitHistoryDetail&type=UnitHistory&ID=160, accessed 10 April 2023

16.   Global Security, Navy ranges, https://www.globalsecurity.org/military/facility/vacapes.htm, accessed 12 April 2023

Frank Wynn Bringard

Corporal · United States Army · Served 1964-1967

Of the Philpott / Bringard line

Frank Wynn Bringard was born on the 3rd of October, 1942 to LaDonna Bringard in Delta, Millard Co., Utah. He was raised in Delta and was drafted to the US Army in 1964.

Wynn entered boot camp at Fort Polk, Louisiana then was transferred to Advanced Infantry Training (AIT) at Fort Leonard Wood, Missouri. After he completed his training, he was assigned to USAG Darmstadt Army Base in Cooperstrasse, Hessa, Germany, which was closed in 2008.

During his tour in Germany, Darmstadt being close to Frankfurt, he attended tasks in Holland and Denmark as well. Wynn was a Combat Engineer, trained for the front lines, building bridges and securing travel for the troops coming up in battle. Having been drafted, his service length was only 2 years and at the end of his duty he was prompted to reenlist but declined.

Image source: Donna Peck

17

Image source: Donna Peck

Wynn was discharged from the Army at Fort Dixon, New Jersey in spring of 1967.

Author Update, 29 March, 2023

In February of 2019, my youngest son, Austin, and I were researching and compiling ancestors' military stories. We wanted to give a memorable birthday gift to my oldest son, Christopher.

During my research, I also wanted to interview and record the accounts of my three living uncles. I had the pleasure of interviewing Uncle Wynn by phone.

The afternoon that I called Uncle Wynn was an opportunity that I'm grateful for. Approximately six weeks later, on Sunday, the 14th of April, 2019, he unexpectedly left this world as the result of a trauma. I had the

FRANK W BRINGARD
SP4 US ARMY
VIETNAM
OCT 3 1942　　APR 14 2019
OUR BELOVED BROTHER
UNCLE AND FRIEND
Image credit: Janice Abbott

privilege of writing his obituary as well as give his eulogy at the funeral. It seems appropriate to share that eulogy here.

Eulogy for
FRANK WYNN BRINGARD
1942 - 2019

Some people knew him as Frank and some knew
him as Wynn. To me he was Uncle Wynn. When
my sister and I were children, we didn't like it if
our parents had Uncle Wynn babysit us. We were
always uncomfortable because he didn't talk much.
In looking back now, the worst thing he did was
to make sure that we stayed in bed at bedtime. He
didn't fall for our bedtime scam of needing to go to
the bathroom three or so times before sleeping. He
was stern, in a child's eyes. Little did I know that he
was the safest babysitter we could have been with. It
wasn't until I became an adult before I realized how
watchful he was over his family.

He made my sister and me leather, horse-shaped
coin purses with our names on the back, which we
both still have and cherish. Working with leather
was not just a hobby to him. It was a part of who he
was. He made beautiful lamps, purses, saddles, belts
and various other articles. Many of his saddles sold
for hundreds of dollars. He made every item with
skill and love, giving most of what he made to those
that he loved. If you received a leather gift from
Uncle Wynn, you just knew that it was his way of
saying "I love you".

Wynn loved horses and had excellent horsemanship,
a skill shared with him from his uncles. As gentle
as he was with people he cared about, I can only
imagine what a great connection he had with the
horses he had when he was younger. He was very

close with his Uncle Sam and his Uncle John as well as always being very devoted to his brothers, Steve and John. He and Steve lived with their grandfather, Frank, until Grandpa's death in 1972. That was a difficult loss for them, as Grandpa Bringard was more like a father to them.

© Kathleen C. Mays

At the beginning of this last March, I had the opportunity to interview Uncle Wynn about his Army service from 1964 to 1967. My son and I were creating a digital book about family members in our genealogical lines who had served at different capacities in the military. I had a whole list of questions for him but with most of the questions, his answer would be, "Aw, hell, I don't remember!" It wasn't until one of my later questions that I understood why I couldn't seem to get much information from him.

When I asked him where he was discharged, he answered and then added, "they wanted me to sign up again and I told them "hell no, I can't get out of here fast enough!" Of the information that I was able to extract from him, maybe you're now sensing why I chose the word EXTRACT, he seemed excited to share that he visited Holland and Denmark. I got the strong impression that he enjoyed these areas. One thing that I'm so grateful for at the end of our conversation is that, for the first time ever, I said, "Uncle Wynn, I sure love you!" He chuckled and said, "oh, (chuckle) love you". We hung up and I called right back and said, "tell Johnny I love him too". He chuckled some more and said ok.

During these last few days, I have heard a similar statement come from several different people. It got me thinking and I point-blank asked my father his opinion. He confirmed what I had been hearing, that no one has ever heard anything harsh or negative said about Uncle Wynn. If I were trying to describe him to someone who had never known him, I would say that he was a quiet, respectful, gentle man, smaller in stature, healthy and strong with blonde hair. His true cowboy roots always colored his dress, grammar and attitude.

He was hard-working and frugal but generous with those he loved. He seemed to take pride in sharing his knowledge with us nieces and nephews. Recently his niece, Teresa, was sewing on her mom's machine when Wynn and Johnny stopped in for a visit. Watching her sew, Wynn related his experiences of sewing leather. Unknown to him, this revived Teresa's childhood desire to work with leather. Early in our lives, he had spent a good deal of time with both her and me, teaching us about this art. She seemed to feel the passion moreso than I.

I'd like to extend immense gratitude to my sister, Teresa, for helping me prepare this verbal tribute to our uncle, a humble and extraordinary man that we were privileged to have in our lives. Bless you Uncle Wynn, as you ride upon greener pastures.

Authored by Kathleen Cary Abbott Mays, the oldest niece of Frank Wynn Bringard

Frank Wynn Bringard died on the 14th of April, 2019 at Delta, Millard Co., Utah, USA.

Sources:

17. Bringard, Frank Wynn, "Details of Wynn Bringard's Military Service," Interview by Kathleen Mays, Military Service of the Abbotts, 12 February 2019

18. Military Bases website, https://militarybases.com/overseas/germany/darmstadt/, viewed 4 Mar /2019, accessed 4 Mar 2019

The United States of America
honors the memory of

Frank Wynn Bringard

This certificate is awarded by a grateful nation in recognition of devoted and selfless consecration to the service of our country in the Armed Forces of the United States.

President of the United States

Image source: U.S. Department of Veterans Affairs

Dale Cary Abbott

Seaman E-3 · United States Navy · Served 1958-1961
Of the Abbott / Cary line

Image source: Dale C. Abbott

Dale Cary Abbott was born on the 3rd of July, 1941 to Lawrence Elnathon & Trula Marie Cary Abbott in Sutherland, Millard Co., Utah. He was raised in the farming community of Sutherland, Utah just a few miles outside of Delta.

Dale entered boot camp on the 7th of July, 1958 at the Naval Training Center in San Diego (NTCSD). He received orders to serve on the USS Midway CVA-41, which was at that time, in dry dock at Hunter's Point, California. When she exited dry dock, a week or two after he received his orders, he and his shipmates were stationed at their stateside home port of Alameda, California.

During his time aboard Midway, he served under Captain J. T. Blackburn in 1958 to 1959, Captain J. H. Mini in 1959 to 1960, Captain RW Cousins in 1960 to 1961 and did a WestPac cruise, visiting Hawaii, The Philippines, Guam, Yokosuka, Japan, which was their overseas home port, and Hong Kong, to name a few.

As Dale described what life was like on board Midway Magic, as

Image source: Dale C. Abbott

Image source: Dale C. Abbott

she is nicknamed, he acknowledged that the food was actually quite good and filling except for some dish they called "SOS". I asked him what that stood for and as he chuckled, he replied "S**t On Shingles". Well Dad, I guess I asked! Actually it is a term to portray the imagery of creamed chipped beef over toast, which apparently was served often.

Interestingly there were similar chuckles during our interview. For example, my question of "what did you do in your leisure time?" received that chuckle, a pause and the answer of "I liked to go to the sponson deck and observe." At this point I decided to be more direct with my questions.

Dale served as Gunner's Mate specializing in artillery, mostly 3 inch and 5 inch gun turrets and mounts. His specific sleeping quarters were midship, one deck below the hangar bay deck and was the only berthing quarters with both port side and starboard side entrances. This area was shared with a number

Image source: Dale C. Abbott

of Marines on-board, serving as personnel control, running the brig, and assisting the Captain.

Dale's service occurred before The United States was formally at war with North Vietnam, although US involvement began as early as 1950 to aid the French. He was not involved in any wartime conflict. On the last leg of their tour, as they were heading stateside, they received orders to shift their destination to Formosa Straits to assist with a conflict. They were en route to Formosa Straits but the orders were cancelled before they arrived.

USS Midway, ca. 1963.

Image source: Wikimedia Commons

The last few months of his service before being discharged on the 13th of November, 1961, he was stationed at NAS Brown Field Chula Vista. A short time later his squadron was transferred to NAS San Diego, North Island due to Brown Field being closed. The Utility Squadron, VU7, had the primary

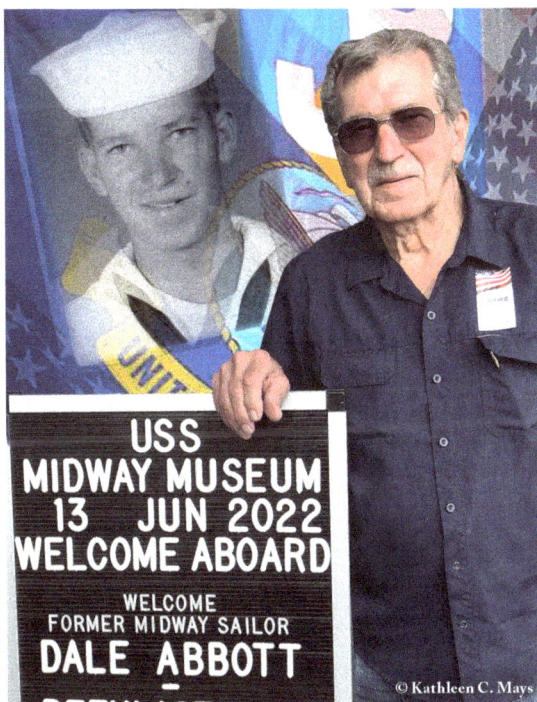

USS
MIDWAY MUSEUM
13 JUN 2022
WELCOME ABOARD

WELCOME
FORMER MIDWAY SAILOR
DALE ABBOTT

© Kathleen C. Mays

© Austin J. Record

Model replica of the USS Midway.

purpose mobilizing targets for practice drills during various ships' General Quarters.

Information is included in this book with permission.

Sources:

19. Abbott, Dale Cary, "Details of Dale Abbott's Military Service," Interview by Kathleen Mays, Military Service of the Abbotts, 4 February 2019

20. Kathleen C. Mays, The USS Midway & Navy Pride, JKabbrisons Photography, https://www.jkabbrisons.com/category/patriotism-military-pride/, documented 12 Sep 2018, accessed 3 Mar 2019, Updated URL, https://jkabbrisons.wixsite.com/jkabbrisonsphotos/post/the-uss-midway-and-navy-pride, accessed 31 March 2023

Lawrence Weston Abbott

2nd Class Petty Officer · United States Navy
Served 1957-1962
Of the Abbott / Cary line

Image credit: Trula Abbott

Lawrence, Neal, Dale, and Navy friend, ca. 1958.

Lawrence Weston Abbott was born on the 16th of February, 1937 to Lawrence Elnathon & Trula Marie Cary Abbott in Delta, Millard Co., Utah. He was raised in the farming community of Sutherland, just a few miles outside of Delta.

Lawrence enlisted for service in the US Navy at Fort Douglas, Utah and reported for boot

Image source: Lawrence Abbott

camp at RTC San Diego. He served from November of 1957 to April of 1962 working as a jet mechanic.

His first 8 months were spent gaining his specialized education at Airman Prep School in Norman, Oklahoma and NATTC Memphis, Tennessee. He was then stationed

Image source: Lawrence Abbott

at NAS Point Mugu, California where he worked a couple of minor assignments.

He promoted up to 2nd Mechanic as a flight crew member on a JD-1D, a propeller driven aircraft that launched target drones from under its wing. He joined VF-154, as as Aviation Machinist Mate Jet (ADJ), aboard the USS Coral Sea CVA-43 after attending

F8U Crusader School at NAS Moffett Field, California.

The F8U is a jet aircraft that Lawrence worked on as a Plane Captain, the assignment of which is performing pre-flight inspections and residing in the cockpit while the jet is on the flight deck until the pilot climbs in for flight. He was also the Maintenance Mechanic.

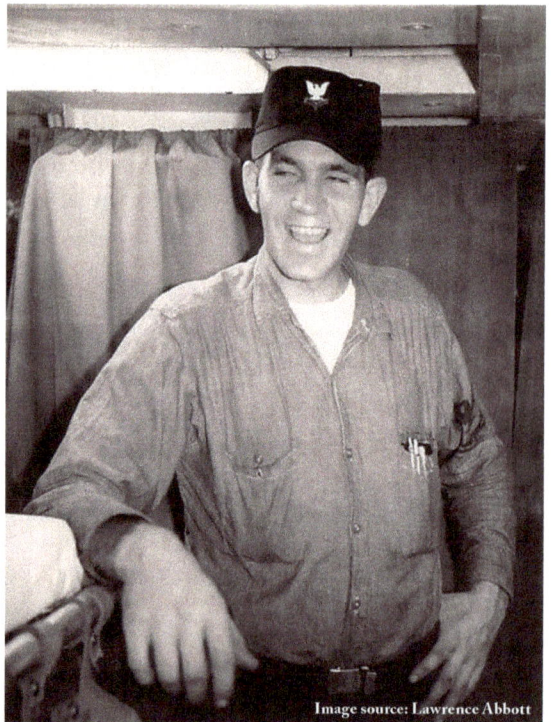

Image source: Lawrence Abbott

USS Coral Sea, ca. 1955.

After their cruise, they headed back to Alameda, California, but they stopped in Hawaii for a few days. In August of 1961, Lawrence's Naval Service was extended due to the closing of the Berlin Wall.

From Alameda, VF-154 was sent to NAS Miramar, California. Lawrence and his fellow Coral Sea shipmates were sent on another WestPac cruise with a repair stop in Yokosuka, Japan where he was separated from his squadron and flew in a super Constellation from Tachikawa AFB to Travis AFB California, with stops in Guam and Hawaii. He was then discharged, with the rank of ADJ-2 (E5), 2nd Class Petty Officer, at Treasure Island, California.

XF3H Demon on USS Coral Sea, ca. 1953.

Information is included in this book with permission.

Sources:

21. Meredith, Laurie Camille Abbott, "Details of Lawrence Abbott's Military Service," Interview by Kathleen Mays, Military Service of the Abbotts, 2 March 2019

22. Abbott, Lawrence Weston, "Details of Lawrence Abbott's Military Service," Interview by Kathleen Mays, Military Service of the Abbotts, 2 March 2019

Military Service in the Abbott Family

Gerald Boone Philpott

Private · United States Army · Served 1941-1945

Of the Philpott / Bringard line

Gerald Boone Philpott was born on the 29th of September, 1924 to John James & Nannie Bell Bryan Philpott in Durham, North Carolina. He enlisted in the US Army and reported for boot camp on the 8th of February, 1941 at Fort Bragg, North Carolina.

Image credit: Weltha Bringard

Gerald and Donna Philpott, ca. 1942.

Image credit: Weltha Bringard

Gerald and Janice Louise Philpott, December 1943.

Gerald was a Private, a member of the 42nd Rainbow Division with Patton's Seventh Army. Entering the service in February 1941, he received his training at Fort Bragg, North Carolina; Fort Douglas, Salt Lake City, Utah; and Fort Custer, Michigan.

He served as Military Police in England and Topaz, Utah, and

Infantry in France and Germany. He was wounded on April 6 in Wurbury, Germany and received a Purple Heart and three Bronze Stars. Gerald was honorably discharged on the 27th of September, 1945.

Gerald Boone Philpott left this world on the 8th of October, 1999 at Mecklenburg, North Carolina, USA.

Sources:

23. "United States World War II Army Enlistment Records, 1938-1946," database, FamilySearch (https://familysearch.org/ark:/61903/1:1:K8L7G1X : 5 December 2014), Gerald B Philpott, enlisted 08 Feb 1941, Ft Bragg, North Carolina, United States; citing "Electronic Army Serial Number Merged File, ca. 1938-1946," database, The National Archives: Access to Archival Databases (AAD) (http://aad.archives.gov : National Archives and Records Administration, 2002); NARA NAID 1263923, National Archives at College Park, Maryland, accessed 22 February 2019

24. "North Carolina, Discharge and Statement of Service Records, 1940-1948," database with images, FamilySearch (https://familysearch.org/ark:/61903/3:1:3QSQ-G9CF-DN5P?cc=2053639&wc=QDY5-THD%3A1589993617 : accessed 3 March 2019), 007387090 > image 360 of 1132; North Carolina State Archives, Raleigh. https://www.familysearch.org LHXD-C7N Notes, 26 August 2013, accessed 3/2/2019

25. Peck, LaDonna Bringard Philpott, as verbalized to Kathleen Cary Abbott Mays about 1987, documented 1987, accessed 23 February 2019

Gerald B Philpott
1924–1999 • LHXD-C7N

▶ Show More

Spouse

La Donna Bringard

Parents

John James Philpott
Nannie Bell Bryan

Gerald B Philpott
United States World War II Army Enlistment Records, 1938-1946

Name:	Gerald B Philpott
Name:	PHILPOTT GERALD B
Event Type:	Military Service
Event Date:	08 Feb 1941
Term of Enlistment:	0
Event Place:	Ft Bragg, North Carolina, United States
Race:	White
Citizenship Status:	citizen
Birth Year:	1922
Birthplace:	NORTH CAROLINA
Education Level:	1 year of high school
Civilian Occupation:	Sales clerks
Marital Status:	Single, without dependents
Military Rank:	Private
Army Branch:	Field Artillery
Army Component:	Regular Army (including Officers, Nurses, Warrant Officers, and Enlisted Men)
Source Reference:	Civil Life
Serial Number:	14039254
Affiliate ARC Identifier:	1263923
Box Film Number:	01492.6

Image source: National Archives and Records Administration

Military Service in the Abbott Family

Image source: Donna Peck

Earl Clark Bringard was born on the 8th of November, 1919 to Frank and Weltha Clark Bringard in Panguitch, Garfield, Utah. He was the 5th of 16 children born to Frank and Weltha.

He was drafted into the US Army after filling out his papers on the 1st of July, 1941 in Delta, Millard, Utah. He was a 5 foot 7 inch, 120 lb. 22 year old man with brown hair and blue eyes.

Earl and Fred Ashby Bennett from Holden, Utah, met the day they reported for duty on the 10th of October, 1941 in Fillmore, Utah. A bus transported them to Fort Douglas in Salt Lake City, Utah.

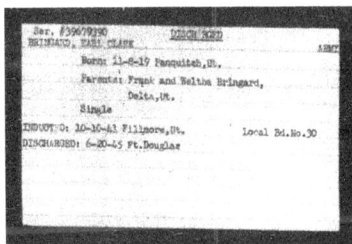

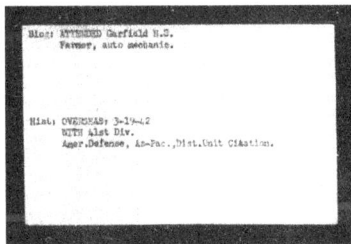

Image source: National Archives at St. Louis, Missouri

As they were talking during the bus ride, they discovered that they both knew Sam McEntyre. That detail solidified the lifelong friendship and the fact that both their surnames began with a 'B' made it easy to be grouped together throughout their assignments.

At Fort Douglas, they received their vaccinations and went through some other preliminary procedures. A few days later they traveled by train to Camp Roberts, located between Monterey and San Luis Obispo in California. Earl and Fred stuck together, becoming known as the "Two Shadows."

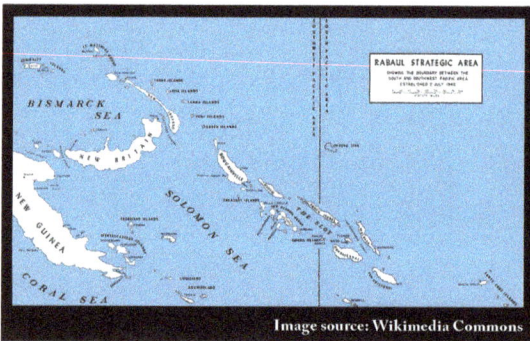

Rabaul Strategic Area

At Camp Roberts, men were chartered from New York, Chicago, and all around the U.S. They were intended to be trained for a year in the areas of firing arms, handling bayonets, hand to hand combat, and a few other fields.

The soldiers were told that anyone who didn't do well at the rifle firing range would have their head shaved right before their two week furlough home for the Christmas holiday. Earl did so well that he was chosen to go to sniper school.

Earl's training at the sniper school only lasted about a week due to the rapidly deteriorating situation with the Japanese enemy. Training was scheduled to take thirteen weeks but ended after only seven weeks.

On the 12th of December, 1941, they were sent by train up the coast to Washington state. The new soldiers were put up to guard the American coastline in case the Japanese attacked the mainland. Part of the squad was assigned to guard the mountain region behind an old C.C.C. camp of the 1930s. (Civilian Conservation Corps)

Earl, Fred, and their fellow soldiers were stationed there in Washington until May of 1942. At this time, they were transported, again by train, to San Francisco, where they boarded the Queen Elizabeth.

The first RMS Queen Elizabeth, which was the sister ship of the Queen Mary, was one of the largest passenger liners ever built. She was launched in 1938 and used as a troopship during World War II.

At this point, rumors suggested that they were going to South America to train or to the Philippines or to several other places. None of these supposed destinations were brought to fruition.

Air raid at Rabaul Harbor, Papua New Guinea.

After eight days of travel on this ship, they woke up, were anchored, and taking on fuel at a French island in the Marquesas group of the South Pacific. After leaving that island, they traveled for three more days into Sydney Harbour.

The soldiers were received kindly, fed, and put on a train to travel to a training area near Melbourne, Australia. It is noted by Fred Bennett that the people were so welcoming, he was left with a desire to visit there again some time later.

Knowing that the Japanese enemy was in New Guinea, having landed on Rabaul on the 23rd of January in 1942, there were concerns that they would attack the Australian coast. Consequently, the American soldiers were sent to the coast just west of New Guinea.

They remained there for several months, until the Japanese had a few reverses. Being shipped to the island, the Americans were sent to a staging area where they awaited orders.

Once the details were decided, the Army flew the soldiers over the Owen Stanley mountain range. Japanese planes flew over the mountain range every morning, so they needed to wait until the Australian troops gave the ok before being flown in light English planes, eight men at a time.

Their unit's primary purpose was to arrive several weeks before the U.S. Marines, to scout the area. The generals and upper ranks implemented the scouts' information to plan their strategy against the Japanese forces.

Landing at a small airfield named Buna, the men proceeded along a coastal road made of logs laid crosswise because of the high tides. As a result of the Americans' placement, they had the Japanese cut off from their main camp.

Private Bringard, Private Bennett, and Private Tom Williams were the main lead scouts when, at approximately 2:00 am on the 21st of January in 1943, eleven Imperial Japanese Marines tried to sneak by the line the Americans held. There were vines and ropes tied to each group of US soldiers so by the time the enemy got to them, they were warned and ready.

Gunfire began once the Japanese were close. Private Fred Bennett recalls, "I remember seeing a muzzle flash from one of their guns and then someone hit me in the left leg with a sledge hammer, I thought. After feeling my leg, I could feel the blood squirting in my hand."

Earl had received powder burns on his face. They killed the rest of the Japanese soldiers and proceeded to put Fred in an old car near the road. One of the enemy killed by Earl was a high ranking officer with a samurai sword. Private

Front cover of Earl's journal.

Bringard captured the sword with its splendid jewels on the hilt, pleased with his dividend. Unfortunately, an unknown comrade found the sword among Earl's personal items, removed, and stole the jewels.

Once daylight came, the Company gave Fred "Sulfa powder" to prevent infection. The last time Fred and Earl saw each other during the war was when the natives came to carry Fred the eight miles to the field hospital where Fred received treatment and survived.

They remained close friends until Earl's death. In fact, Earl's youngest son was named Fred in honor of Private Bennett.

United States Army Private Earl C. Bringard suffered through the serious disease of malaria, earned a silver star, 3 battle ribbons, and was nominated for a congressional medal. He was also well-known as the top marksman in the area.

During his service, an Army buddy of Earl's, a young Lakota Sioux man, Phillips, etched the artwork design on Earl's metal journal cover. The journal is safely kept by his son Dan, who has graciously shared the images of it. We are fortunate in that these images reveal Earl's handwriting and innermost thoughts. He even recorded the serial number of his rifle. We are also including a transcription.

Back cover of Earl's journal.

All grammar reflects Earl's original text. Punctuation has been added for ease of reading.

PM/M day
2/6
Earl C. Bringard 39679390
Earl C. Bringard
Rifel no.
98002

Upon a windswept plateau and what a hell of a spot; Battling terrible dust storms in the land that Time forgot; Into the brush with a rifle, down in a ditch with a pick; Doing the work of negroes and too damn tired to kick; Up with the cowboys and Indians, up where a man gets blue; Up near the tops of the mountains and thousands of miles from you; At night the wind keeps howling, it's more than a man can't stand; Hell no we're not convicts, we're defenders of our land; We are living for tomorrow, only to see our gals; Hoping that when we do return, they're not married to our pals; We are soldiers of selective ser[*vice*], earning our meager pay; Guarding the wallstreet mills, for less than a buck a day; No one knows we are living, nobody gives a damn;

Back home we are soon forgotten, we're loaned to Uncle Sam; Only one year we can stand it, one year from our lives we'll miss Boys don't let the army get you, and for hell's sake don't re-enlist.

pm/m dd
2/6
Earl C. Bringard 39477390

Earl C. Bringard
Rifel no.
98002

Image credit: Dan Bringard

Earl Clark Bringard

Upon a wind swept plateau
and what a hell of a spot
Battling terrible duststorms
In the land that time forgot
Into the brush with a rifle
down in a ditch with a pick
doing the work of negroes
and too damned tired to kick
up with the cowboys and Indians
up where a man gets blue
up near the tops of the mountains
and thousands of miles from you
at night the wind keeps howling
It's more than a man can stand
Hell no we're not convicts
we're defenders of our land
We are living for tomorrow
Only to see our gals
Hoping that when we do return
they're not married to our pals
We are soldiers of selective service
earning our meager pay
Guarding the wall street millions
for less than a buck a day.
No one knows we are living
Nobody gives a damn.

Military Service in the Abbott Family

Back home we are soon forgotten
We're loaned to Uncle Sam
Only one year we can stand it
one year fron our lives we'll miss
Boys dont let the army get you
and for hell's sake dont
                    ye'enlist

There's usually a counterattack, they thrust right back at you, but when you beat them off again and there's nothing left to do, the captain comes around and says there's mail for you. As you glance through a letter, from your loved one so dear, and you find she's forgotten you, it's hard to hold that tear. After you get to thinking, you find it's for the best. The girl she didn't love you and worry's off your chest. By Earl Bringard

In the state of old Utah near the top of the peak, white clouds struck. Its shadows in a draw where green trees grow and the cool breezes blow. In the state of old Utah the rolling hills and old saw mills, it's a site all man should see. The fishing streams, it all means, a life of luxury. The green grass lands and the desert sands, is my old home, just to be there, in the open so fair, I never want to name.

I wouldn't change my food with a city dude. My clothes are so plain, my pants are torn, my shaps are worn, they won't hold out the rain. But I want to go back to that old ranch shack and hear the old crows caw, at my home, my old, sweet home in the state of old Utah. By E. C. Bringard.

Theres usualy a counter alact
they thrust right back
    at you.

But when you beat them
    of agen
and theres nothing lift to do
the captan comes around
and says theres mail
    for you

As you glance thrugh a
    letter
from your loved one so
    dear
And you find shes forgotten you
Its hard to hold that tear
after you get to thinking
you find its for the best
the girl she didnt love
    you
and the worrys off your
    chest.
        By
    E. C. Bringard

In the state of old Utah
near the tops of the peak
white clouds struck
its shadows in a draw
wher green trees grow
and the cool breezes blow
In the state of old Utah
The rolling hills and
old saw milles
its a sight all man should see
The fishing streams
it all means
A life of luxure
The green grass lands
and the desert sands
is my old home range
just to be there
in the open so fair
I never wont to change
range

Military Service in the Abbott Family

I wouldn't change my food
my old ranch food
with a city dude
my cloths are so plane
my pants are torn
my shaps are worn
They wont holdout the
rain

But I wont to go back
to that old ranch shak
And here the old crows caw
at my home my old sweet
home
in the state of old Utah

By
E. C. Bringard

RFG [or C] Fred Bennett
105 General Hospital APO 923

As long as life

As long as rivers run their course, as long as skies
are blue, and just as long as I have breath, I shall
remember you —- I shall remember all the words
—- you ever said to me —- the plans we made
together one —- when we were young and free —- I
shall remember how you looked —- in purple and
in brown —- where are you preferred my company
—- to other men —- in town, I shall remember how
you smiled —- with eyes that wondered why —- I
seemed to be in love with you —- yet sometimes
passed you by —- and just as long as there is life —-
and there are night and day —- I shall remember
and regret —- the time I went away.

My girl

I'd like to tell you what I think of a girl I know
so well, although I haven't seen her, she's a darling
I can tell. She writes to me so often and tells me all
the news and if I ever have a date, she's the one I'll
choose. You see I'm very much in love with her and
her eyes of brown. I think that she's a sweetest one
of any girl in town. She has black hair that I adore,
her clothes are worn so neat, her lips are very nice
indeed and her smile is O so sweet. I often wondered
what she thinks of me so far away. I'm hoping that
she feels the same and asked me home to stay.

Dear folks

Can't write a thing the censors to blame —-
just say that I'm well and sign my name. Can't
tell where we sail from, can't mention the date,
can't even mention the meals I ate —- can't say
where I'm going, don't know where I'll land —-
can't even inform you if met by a band —- can't
mention the weather can't say if there's rain —- all
military secrets, must secrets remain —- can't have
a flashlight to guide me at night —- can't smoke a
cigarett except out of sight —- can't keep a diary for
such is a sin —- can't keep the envelopes your letters
came in —- can't say for sure now just what I can
write —- so I'll close the letter and say good night.
I'll send you this letter to say that I'm well —- still
grumbling and growling and fighting like hell.

PFC. Fred A. Burnett
105 General Hospital A.P.O. 923

As long as life

as long as rivers run their
course.... As long as skies
are blue — I shall remember
and just as long as I have
breath — I shall remember
you — I shall remember all
the words — you ever said
to me — The Plans we made
together once — when we
were young & free — I
shall remember how you
looked — in purple and
in brown — when you
Preferred my company —
to other men in town —
I shall remember how you
smiled — with eyes

that wondered why --- I seemed
to be in love with you ---
yet sometimes passed you
by --- and just as long
as there is life --- and
there are night & day ---
I shall remember and regret
--- the time I went away.

My girl

I'd like to tell you what I think
of a girl I know so well
Although I haven't met seen her
she's a darling I can tell

She writes to me so often
and tells me all the news
And if I ever have a date
she's the one I'll choose

I you see I'm very much in love
With her and her eyes of brown
I think that she's the sweetest one
of any girl in town

she has black hair that I adore
her clothy are worn so neat
her lips are very nice indeed
and her smile is O so sweet
I often wondered what she thinks
of me so far away
I'm hoping that she feels th same
and askes me home to stay.

Dear Folks ⟶

Cant write a thing the censors
to blame --- Just say that
I'm well and sign my name
Cant tell where we sail
from cant mention the date
Cant even mention the
meals I ate --- Cant say
where I'm going don't know
where I'll land --- Can't even
inform you if met by a
band --- Cant mention

Military Service in the Abbott Family

The weather cant say if there
rain --- All military secrets
must secrets remain ---
Cant have a flashlight
to guide me at night ---
Cant smoke a cigaret
except out of sight ---
Cant keep a diary for sure
is a sin --- Cant keep
the envelopes your letters
came in --- Cant say for
sure now just what I can
write --- So Ill close this
letter and say good night
Ill send you this letter
to say that I'm well ~
still grumbling and
growling and fighting
like hell.

Earl Clark Bringard   53

Image credit: Amber Minchey

He died on the 25th of November in 1969 at Hurricane, Washington Co., Utah, USA, having suffered through many years of post-traumatic stress disorder or PTSD.

Sources:

26. "Utah, World War II Index to Army Veterans of Utah, 1939-1945," database, <i>FamilySearch</i> (https://www.familysearch.org/ark:/61903/1:1:73KN-MTN2 : 30 June 2020), Bringard Earl Clark, 10 Oct 1941; citing Military Service, Fillmore, Millard, Utah, United States, Utah State Archives, Salt Lake City; FHL microfilm 008244948. Accessed 28 March, 2023

Image credit: Amber Minchey

27. Bringard, Dan, son, "Details of Earl Clark Bringard's Military Service," Interview by Kathleen Mays, Military Service of the Abbotts, 11 April 2023

28. Wikipedia, The Free Encyclopedia, "Battle of Rabaul (1942)," https://en.wikipedia.org/wiki/Neutralisation_of_Rabaul, accessed 15 April 2023

29. Bringard, Earl Clark, "Journal of Private Earl C. Bringard" ca. 1941 - 45, in possession of Dan Bringard, accessed 11 April 2023

30. Brittanica, "Queen Elizabeth, British Passenger Ships," Written and fact-checked by, The Editors of Encyclopaedia Britannica, Last Updated: Apr 7, 2023, https://www.britannica.com/topic/Queen-Elizabeth-British-passenger-ships, accessed 30 April 2023.

31. Bennett, Fred Ashby, Letter of July 12, 2001 to Dan Bringard, copied and mailed, accessed 29 April, 2023

Samuel Bennett Abbott

Private · United States Army · Served 1943-1944

Of the Abbott / Cary line

Samuel Bennett Abbott was born on the 19th of January, 1919 to Edward Lawrence and Josephine Bennett Abbott in Sutherland, Millard Co., Utah.

He enlisted in the United States Army on the 17th of November, 1943 for the duration of World War II. He is reported to have been in Lassen, California shortly thereafter although I do not know the specifics, whether it was a training facility or not.

Image source: Dale Abbott

Bennett was killed at LaSalle, Le Vigan, Gard, Languedoc-Roussillon, France on the 31st of October, 1944, reportedly by machine gun fire while helping injured soldiers.

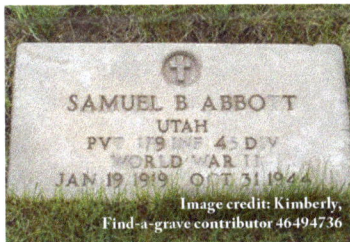

Image credit: Kimberly, Find-a-grave contributor 46494736

He was serving as a medic in the 179th Infantry, 45th Division. Although the family was notified of his death, they did not receive his body for burial until the 31st of July, 1948. Bennett's grave is at the Delta City Cemetery.

His nephew, Dale, recollected that Edward Lawrence, Bennett's father, and Lawrence Elnathon, Bennett's older brother, question the legitimacy of the reports. Apparently they were initially told that there was not a body left to bury, that Bennett was completely disorganized by mortar explosions. When they received his remains approximately 4 years later, they were left wondering if it was even Bennett's remains.

Ser. # 39922572   KILLED - BODY RETURNED TO UT.
ABBOTT, SAMUEL B., Pvt.   7-9-48 FOR RE-BURIAL ARMY
   (medical corps)
   Born:
   Parents: Mr. and Mrs. Edward Lawrence Abbott
       Delta, Utah
   Wife: Mrs. Mona Young Abbott, Idaho Falls, Idaho
      daughter, Patricia
     Entered: a yr. ago
   KILLED SERVING WITH MEDICAL CORPS IN EUROPEAN AREA (Trib.
   11-25-44)
     Reported: 12-9-44

Image source: National Archives and Records Administration

Before reading on, in Bennett's Last Action Report, note that each page looks as though it has been partially burned. Indeed, they were in The National Personnel Records Center fire of 1973.

This fire occurred at the Military Personnel Records Center (MPRC) in St. Louis, Missouri, on July 12, 1973. The MPRC lost approximately 16–18 million official military personnel records as a result of the fire. For an interesting read, search in Wikipedia or go to the link: https://en.wikipedia.org/wiki/National_Personnel_Records_Center_fire

RE: _abbott, Samuel B._   _39 927 572_

THE REPLY TO THE INQUIRY WILL BE FOUND IN THE CHECKED ITEM(S). IF YOU WRITE TO US AGAIN ON THIS SUBJECT, PLEASE RETURN YOUR ORIGINAL REQUEST, THIS FORM, AND ANY OTHER FORM YOU COMPLETE.

[X] Copies of requested military [X] personnel [X] medical   records are attached. We suggest you make an extra copy and guard against loss or damage. We regret if any photocopies may be of poor quality, but they are the best copies obtainable. _½ Php/52 -1/503/3 citation_

[ ] The attached separation document may include the following information: authority for separation, reason for separation, Reenlistment Eligibility Code, and Separation (SPN/SPD) Code. If you require a copy of the separation document that does not contain the above information, you may request a deleted copy from this Center.

[ ] The Privacy Act of 1974 does not permit the release of a social security number or other personal information to the public without the authorization of the veteran concerned; therefore, we have deleted personal identifying data relating to other persons.

[ ] The record of service in the _____ indicates being in a POW status from _____ to _____

[ ] When the person named above was separated, it was not the practice to issue a document which served as a report of separation.

[ ] The original Report of Separation was issued at the time of separation. Another original cannot be issued. The attached copy, however, will serve the same purpose as the original.

[ ] No Report of Separation was issued since the person named above had no active service, or less than 90 days of active duty for training.

[ ] The service record of the person named above does not contain a copy of a Report of Separation, or its equivalent. Therefore, we are instead furnishing the attached NA Form 13038, Certification of Military Service. This will serve as verification of military service and may be used for any official purpose.

[ ] The record needed to answer your inquiry was filed in the area that suffered the most damage in a fire here on July 12, 1973, and was damaged/partially destroyed. The specific document or information requested was not contained in the records that were recovered from the burned area.

[ ] The record needed to answer your inquiry is not in our files. If the record were here on July 12, 1973, it would have been in the area that suffered the most damage in the fire on that date and may have been destroyed.

Fortunately, alternate records sources often contain information that can be used to reconstruct service record data lost in the fire.

[ ] The information used to prepare the attached NA Form 13038, Certification of Military Service, was obtained from an alternate records source. This certificate will serve as verification of military service and may be used for any official purpose.

[ ] The enclosed copies of documents were obtained from an alternate records source.

[ ] However, complete records cannot be reconstructed.

[ ] However, we regret that these sources do not contain the particular type of information or document requested.

[ ] We will attempt to obtain the required information from these alternate records sources if you will assist us by completing the attached NA Form 13075, Questionnaire About Military Service, to the best of your ability.

[ ] In attempting to provide information from alternate records sources concerning illness or injury while in military service, we need additional information as to the approximate dates of illness or injury and the specific organization assignments (company, battalion, regiment, division, group, etc.) at that time. Please complete the attached NA Form 13055, to the best of your ability.

When we receive the necessary data we shall promptly make every effort to reconstruct the requested information, using the resources available.

[X] That portion of your request seeking medals/awards has been referred to the office checked below. That office has jurisdiction over the issuance of medals/awards. Any further correspondence on this subject should be addressed to that office.

[X] ARPERCEN, Attn: DARP-PAS-EAW   [ ] Navy Liaison Office, Room 3475, N-314   9700 Page Blvd., St. Louis, MO 63132-5100

[ ] The medical records you request   [ ] The documents you request pertaining to discharge   have been lent to the Department of Veterans Affairs (VA) and may be obtained from the VA office shown below.

[ ] The Department of Defense Privacy Program, 32 CFR 286a.30(f), allows for the disclosure of medical records to the individual to whom they pertain. A portion of your medical records, however, contain information which can be interpreted and explained properly only by a physician. If you wish us to send copies to a designated physician, please furnish us with the name and address of that physician. The request MUST INCLUDE the written consent (signature) of the person whose records are involved, authorizing the release of the records to the designated physician.

[ ]

Neal Abbott
3755 West 2500 North
Delta, UT 84624

NCPM _RM/RLebret_

WILLIAM D. BASSMAN
Chief, Records Reconstruction Branch

NATIONAL PERSONNEL RECORDS CENTER
(Military Personnel Records)
9700 Page Boulevard
St. Louis, Missouri 63132-5100

NATIONAL ARCHIVES AND RECORDS ADMINISTRATION   NA FORM 13045 (REV 9-90)

WAR DEPARTMENT
THE ADJUTANT GENERAL'S OFFICE
WASHINGTON 25, D. C.

REPORT OF DEATH

DATE 27 Nov 1944

rm 4627

FULL NAME	ARMY SERIAL NUMBER	GRADE
Abbott, Samuel B.	39 922 572	Pvt.

HOME ADDRESS	ARM OR SERVICE	DATE OF BIRTH
Bieber, Calif.	Medical Dept.	19 Jan 1919

PLACE OF DEATH	CAUSE OF DEATH	DATE OF DEATH
European Area	Killed in action	31 Oct 44

STATION OF DECEASED	DATE OF ENTRY ON CURRENT ACTIVE SERVICE	LENGTH OF SERVICE FOR PAY PURPOSES
European Area	17 Nov 1943	YEARS / MONTHS / DAYS

EMERGENCY ADDRESSEE (NAME, RELATIONSHIP & ADDRESS)

Mrs. Mona Young Abbott, wife, 549 North Water Ave., Idaho Falls, Idaho

BENEFICIARY (NAME, RELATIONSHIP & ADDRESS)

Mrs. Mona Young Abbott, wife, address above.
Patricia Irene Abbott, daughter, Delta, Utah
Mr. Edward Lawrence Abbott, father, Delta, Utah &

INVESTIGATION MADE?		IN LINE OF DUTY		OWN MISCONDUCT		WAS DECEASED ON DUTY STATUS		AUTHORIZED ABSENCE		IN FLYING PAY STATUS		OTHER PAY STATUS (SPECIFY BELOW)	
YES	NO	YES	NO	YES	NO	YES	NO	YES	NO	YES	NO	YES	NO
											X		X

ADDITIONAL DATA AND/OR STATEMENT

Mrs. Josephine Bennett Abbott, mother, Delta, Utah.

    The individual named in this report of death is held by the War Department to have been in a missing in action status from 31 Oct 44, until such absence was terminated on 17 Nov 44, when evidence considered sufficient to establish the fact of death was received by the Secretary of War from the Commanding General of the European Area.

FILE IN
DEMOBILIZED PERSONNEL REC...

NOV 29 44 F...

COPIES FURNISHED:				
S. S. O.	F. B. L.	F. O., U. S. A.	X	BATTLE
S. O. O. M. G.	O. F. D.	ARMY EFFECTS BUREAU CASUALTY BRANCH FILE		NON-BATTLE
G. A. O.	VET. ADMIN.	A. B. 201 FILE		

WD, AGO, FORM NO. 52-1, 29 MAY 1944

PD-R

THE ADJUTANT GENERAL'S OFFICE
WASHINGTON D. C.

20 Dec. 1944

Last Name — First Name — Middle Initial		Army Serial No.	Grade	
Abbott Samuel B.		39 921 972	Pvt.	Engrave and Ship
Organization	Component	Foreign	Others	
Medical M. Dept.				
Headquarters		G. O. No. Section	Date of Orders	
Type of Award		Posthumous Deluxe Duplicate		
M				
By Command of		Rescinded	Revoked	Amended	Corrected Copy
Citation Station and Date		Present Station if Living; Otherwise Present Status		
Next of Kin (Name and Address)				

BY ORDER OF THE SECRETARY OF WAR

Mrs. Mona Young Abbott
549 North Water Avenue
Idaho Falls, Idaho.

J. A. ULIO

Adjutant General

CITATION

W.D. AGO Form No. 0712
August 1944

WAR DEPARTMENT
THE ADJUTANT GENERAL'S OFFICE
WASHINGTON D.C

NOTICE AND RECORD OF AWARD OF DECORATION

Last Name — First Name — Middle Initial		Army Serial No.	Grade		
Abbott, Samuel L.		3. 695 572	Pvt.	Entered and Grade	
Organization	Component	Foreign	Others		
Medical Department					
Headquarters		S O No. Section	Date of Orders		
45th Inf. Div.		192	22 May 45		
Type of Award		Posthumous	Oak-Leaf Clusters	Number	Posthumous
Bronze Star Medal		Yes			
By Command of		Rescinded	Revoked	Amended	Corrected Copy
Citation Station and Date		Present Station If Living Otherwise Present Status			
		Killed in action			
Next of Kin (Name and Address) Mrs. Nola L. Abbott 545 North Water Avenue Idaho Falls, Idaho	Relationship Wife	Presentation To Be Made By Commanding General Ninth Service Command Fort Douglas, Utah			

BY ORDER OF THE SECRETARY OF WAR

W. H. FALLON

JUL 2 4 1945
Adjutant General

CITATION

ABBOTT, SAMUEL B.

45th Inf Div   APO 45

BRONZE STAR MEDAL   YES

Order Number	Serial Number	Grade
General 191	39923978	Pvt
Posthumous	31 May 45	

For heroic achievement in action on 31 October 1944 near LaSalle, France. The enemy directed continuous and heavy mortar fire on the positions of a rifle company, inflicting a large number of casualties. Private Abbott, in spite of the heavy mortar and small arms fire covering the area, left his foxhole and moved through the impact area from one wounded man to another rendering first aid. He had succeeded in administering to the needs of four of the wounded and was moving on the fifth when he was hit, and killed by fire from an enemy machine gun. The prompt medical attention rendered by Private Abbott undoubtedly saved the lives of these men. His courage and devotion to duty reflect great credit upon himself and his organization.

Next of Kin: Mr. Edward L. Abbott, (father), Delta, Utah.

THE ADJUTANT GENERAL'S OFFICE. DECORATIONS AND AWARDS BRANCH. WASHINGTON. D. C.
RECORD OF AWARD OF DECORATION

FILE IN ENLISTED

OFFICIAL STATEMENT of the MILITARY SERVICE and DEATH

of

SAMUEL B. ABBOTT

Army Serial Number 39 922 572

The official records show that Samuel B. Abbott, Army serial number 39 922 572, was inducted into the military service 17 November 1943 at Salt Lake City, Utah, at which time he gave his home address as Bieber, California. He was killed in action 31 October 1944 in France, while serving as a private.

This official statement of the military service and death furnished 26 June 1947 to Roy C. Coles, General Delivery, Rigby, Idaho.

BY AUTHORITY OF THE SECRETARY OF WAR:

Countersigned

EDWARD F. WITSELL
Major General
The Adjutant General

Adjutant General

Image source: Neal Abbott per National Archives and Records Administration

REPORT OF 18 Dec 1943
PHYSICAL EXAMINATION AND INDUCTION

First examination ☒   Second examination   Third examination   Fourth examination
(To be filled in by local board clerk. Check number of examination made by local board)

SECTION I.—GENERAL (To be filled in by the local board clerk from the Selective Service Questionnaire, D. S. S. Form 40. Where appropriate the questions where no information is given. Do not leave any question)

To be filled in by Armed Forces	In the State Assigned in This Column
	Examination
	State

1. Name (page 1) ..... SAMUEL (First) BENNETT (Middle) ABBOTT (Last) .....

County

2. Address (page 1) ..... BIEBER (Town or city) ..... CALIFORNIA (County) (State)

Place Inducted

3. Social Security No. (Series I, line 5) 528-18-6904   4. Registrant's order number (page 1) 645

5. Physical or mental defects or diseases (Series II, line 1) None

Date Inducted

6. Treatment at an institution, sanitarium, or asylum. Series II, line 2 No

7. Education (Number years completed) (Series III) : Elementary school 8 High school 3 Vocational school, college, or university

Month

8. Occupation: (a) Title of present job (Series IV, line 2 (a), or Series V, Line 1 Work in Saw Mill

(b) Duties (Series IV, line 2 (b)) Kailing of a Re-Saw in a saw mill

Year

(c) Title of last job, if unemployed (Series IV, line 3)

9. Years experience in this work (Series IV, line 2 (c), or Series V, line c) 1 Mo.

10. Income (Series IV, line 2 (d)): Average Weekly (Weekly, monthly, annual) earnings $1.20

11. Employment class (Series IV, line 2 (f)): Permanent employee ☐; Temporary employee ☒; Apprentice ☐; Independent worker ☐
Unpaid family worker ☐; Employer ☐; Student (Series IV, line 4 (a)) ☐

12. Business of present employer (Series IV, line 2 (g)) Saw Mill

13. Marital status (Series VII, line 1): Single ☐; Widower ☐; Divorced ☐; Married, not separated ☒; Married, separated ☐

14. Number of dependents (Series VII, line 3 (c) fifth column except N. C.'s plus line 4 (a) fifth column) One

15. Birthplace (Series IX, line 1) SUTHERLAND (Town or city) UTAH (State) U.S.A. (Country)

16. Birth date (Series IX, line 2) January (Month) 19 (Day) 1919. (Year)

17. Race (Series IX, line 3): White ☒; Negro ☐; Other (specify)

18. Citizenship: United States citizen (Series IX, line 4) Yes (Yes or no); Declarant alien (Series IX

19. Previous U. S. military service (Series XII): None ☒; Army ☐; National Guard ☐; Navy ☐

20. Type of discharge (Series XII): Specify

21. Date of registrant's affidavit (top of page 8) 6th (Day) May (Month)

INSTRUCTIONS
1. An original and three copies of this form will be prepared is designated as the Armed Forces' Original; the first copy Surgeon General's (Army)—Bureau of Medicine copy, the Local Board's Copy

39. Eye abnormalities _____ none

40. Ear, nose, throat abnormalities _____ none

41. Mouth and gum abnormalities _____ none
Class III

42. Teeth: (a) Indicate restorable carious teeth by circling; nonrestorable carious teeth by /; missing natural teeth by X.

	Right								Examiner's					Left			
1	7	6	5	4	3	2	1	1	2	3	4	5	6	7	8	
16	15	14	13	12	11	10	9	9	10	11	12	13	14	15	16	

(b) Remarks, including other defects _____ none

(c) Prosthetic dental appliances _____ none

(d) Remediable dental defects _____ none

43. Skin _____ normal
44. Varicose veins _____ none

45. Hernia _____ none

46. Hemorrhoids _____ none

47. Genito-urinary (non-venereal) _____ normal

48. Venereal diseases _____ none .

49. Feet _____ normal

50. Musculoskeletal defects _____ none

51. Abdominal viscera _____ normal

52. Cardiovascular system _____ normal

53. Lungs _____ normal

54. Chest X-ray #62942 No Disqualifying Abnormalities.

55. Mental _____ normal

56. Nervous system _____ normal

57. Endocrine system _____ normal
58. Other defects and/or diseases or other remarks _____ XXX

60. Vision without correction:
(a) Right eye _20/20_
(b) Left eye _20/20_
61. Vision with correction:
(a) Right eye _____
(b) Left eye _____
62. Color perception* _____
63. Hearing:
(a) Right ear _15/15_
(b) Left ear _15/15_
64. Height _70_ inches.
65. Weight _150_ pounds.
66. (a) Girth, at nipples, inspiration _____ inches.
(b) Girth, at nipples, expiration _35_ inches.
(c) Girth, at umbilicus _35½_ inches.
67. Posture:
Good ☐ Fair ☒ Poor ☐
68. Frame:
Heavy ☐ Med. ☒ Light ☐
69. Color of hair _Brn_
70. Color of eyes _Blue_
71. Complexion _Ruddy_
72. Pulse, sitting _80_
73. Pulse, after exercise* _____
74. Pulse, 3 minutes after exercise* _____
75. Blood pressure:
(a) Systolic _130_
(b) Diastolic _76_
76. Urinalysis:
(a) Specific gravity _1.022_
(b) Albumin _none_
(c) Sugar _____
(d) Microscopic _____
77. Other data _____

Image source: Neal Abbott per National Archives and Records Administration

(b) Do you find that the above-named registrant has any of the defects set forth in Part II
(If in doubt, answer "no," and give details.) __no__ If answer is "yes," describe the
(Answer yes or no)

(c) I have examined the above-named registrant in accordance with Selective Service Regulations.

(d) Signature of examining physician ....

(e) Place __Bieber__ __Lassen__ __Calif.__ Date __11-25-42__
(Town or city) (County) (State)

27. (a) This Local Board has classified the above-named registrant in Class __1-A__

(b) Signature of Member of Local Board .... (d) Date ....
(Town or city) (County) (State)

SECTION III.—NEAREST RELATIVE, PERSON TO BE NOTIFIED IN CASE OF EMERGENCY, AND DESIGNATION OF
BENEFICIARY (To be filled out at the induction station of the armed forces for only those registrants accepted for military service)

A. Nearest relative and person to be notified in case of emergency:

28. Nearest relative __Edward Lawrence Abbott__
(Other than wife or minor child. Name in full)

29. Relationship __Father__ 30. Address __None__ __Delta, Utah__
(Number and street or rural route; if none, so state) (City, town, or post office) (State or country)

31. Person to be notified in case of emergency __Iona Young Abbott__
(Name in full)

32. Relationship __Wife__ 33. Address __None__ __Delta, Utah__
(If friend, so state) (Number and street or rural route; if none, so state) (City, town, or post office) (State or country)

B. Designation of beneficiary:

34. The persons eligible to be my beneficiary are designated below:

(1) __Iona Young Abbott__ __(Wife)__ __Delta, Utah__
(Full name of wife; if no wife, or if she is deceased or divorced, so state) (Wife's full address)

(2) __Patricia Irene Abbott__ __(Daughter)__ __Same address__
(Full name and address of each minor child and each dependent child over 21 years of age. If there are no children, so state. If the address is the same as the

__XX__
wife's, so state. Do not repeat address)

35. In the event of my leaving no widow or child, or their decease before payment is made, I then designate as my beneficiary the
dependent relative whose name, relationship, and address are shown below:

(3) __Edward Lawrence Abbott__ __Father__ __Delta, Utah__
(If designation of beneficiary is declined, he must state in own handwriting: "I desire to decline any person to be the

36. In the event of the death or disqualification of the last-named dependent relative before payment is made, I then designate as
my beneficiary the dependent relative whose name, relationship, and address are shown below:

(4) __Josephine Bennett Abbott__ __Mother__ __Delta, Utah__
(If beneficiary is named in line 35 but naming of alternate is declined, man must state in own handwriting: "I decline to designate an alternate beneficiary")

37. Signature of registrant __Sam__ __B__ __Abbott__
(First name) (Middle name) (Last name)

38. Witnessed at __Salt Lake City, Utah__ on __17 Nov 1943__, 19

.... __B. M. HARRINGTON__ __1st Lt., AGD__
(Signature of witness attesting) (Name of witness typed) (Grade and organization)

ORIGINAL COPY (PAGE 2) o16—26941-2

Samuel Bennett Abbott 65

Image source: Neal Abbott per National Archives and Records Administration

reason of _____

_____

(d) _____ is physically qualifi[...]
       (Enter name of registrant if this subsection is applicable)

satisfactory correction of the following remediable defects: _____

_____

This registrant would have been acceptable for limited military service had the remediable defects herei[...] at the time of this examination.

(e) _____ is physically and/or mentally disqualified for military
       (Enter name of registrant if this subsection is applicable)

_____

(f) _____ is disqualified for military service because of _____
       (Enter name of registrant if this subsection is applicable)

_____

(g) Signature ~~_____~~ (h) Title __Captain, M. C.__
                                   Medical Examiner.

(i) Name typed or stamped   LEON M. SWIFT

79. (a)   **Samuel Bennett Abbott** _____ was this date inducted for (general, ~~limited~~) [strike out inapplicable
          (Enter name of registrant if this subsection is applicable)
       word] military service into the (fill in appropriate Service, such as Army, Navy, Marine Corps, or Coast Guard) _____
       Army _____ of the United States and sent to Recpt. Ctr. Ft. Douglas, Utah _____

(b) _____ was this date rejected for service in the (fill in appropriate
       (Enter name of registrant if this subsection is applicable)

       service, such as Army, Navy, Marine Corps, or Coast Guard) _____ of the United States.
(c) Place Salt Lake City, Utah _____ (d) Signature _____
(e) Date 17 Nov 1943 (f) Name typed or stamped B. M. HARRINGTON, 1st Lieut., A.G.D.
                                                                      (Grade and organization)

SECTION V.—LOCAL BOARD CHANGE IN CLASSIFICATION AFTER EXAMINATION BY THE INDUCTION STATION OF THE ARMED FORCES.

80. (a) Based on the entries in (a), (c), (d), (e), or (f) of Item 78, above, the Local Board has changed the above-named registrant's classification to Class _____
    (b) Based on the entries in (b) of Item 78, above, the Local Board has retained the above-named registrant in Class _____
    (c) Place _____ (d) Date _____
    (e) Signature of member of local board _____

FINGERPRINTS—RIGHT HAND

1. THUMB	2. INDEX	3. MIDDLE	4. RING	5. LITTLE

ORIGINAL COPY   (PAGE 4)   e16—29041-2   U. S. GOVERNMENT PRINTING OFFICE

Image source: Neal Abbott per National Archives and Records Administration

DARP-PAS-EAW
Abbott, Samuel B.   39 922 572
jj/2/18/2

DEPARTMENT OF THE ARMY
ARPERCEN
ST. LOUIS, MISSOURI 63132-5200
AUTHORIZATION FOR ISSUANCE OF AWARDS

TO:	Commander US Army Support Activity Philadelphia, PA 19101	DATE 10 June 1991

CODE NUMBERS FOR AWARDS

1	MEDAL OF HONOR	14	PURPLE HEART	27	NATIONAL DEFENSE SERVICE MEDAL
2	DISTINGUISHED SERVICE CROSS	15	GOOD CONDUCT MEDAL	28	KOREAN SERVICE MEDAL
3	DEFENSE DISTINGUISHED SERVICE MEDAL	16	PRESIDENTIAL UNIT EMBLEM	29	ANTARTICA SERVICE MEDAL
4	DISTINGUISHED SERVICE MEDAL	17	MERITORIOUS UNIT EMBLEM	30	ARMED FORCES EXPEDITIONARY MEDAL
5	SILVER STAR	18	VALOROUS UNIT EMBLEM	31	VIETNAM SERVICE MEDAL
6	LEGION OF MERIT	19	WOMEN'S ARMY CORPS SERVICE MEDAL	32	ARMED FORCES RESERVE MEDAL
7	DISTINGUISHED FLYING CROSS	20	AMERICAN DEFENSE SERVICE MEDAL	33	ARMY RESERVE COMPONENTS ACHIEVEMENT MEDAL
8	SOLDIER'S MEDAL	21	AMERICAN CAMPAIGN MEDAL	34	COMBAT INFANTRYMAN BADGE
9	BRONZE STAR MEDAL	22	ASIATIC-PACIFIC CAMPAIGN MEDAL	35	EXPERT INFANTRYMAN BADGE
10	MERITORIOUS SERVICE MEDAL	23	EUROPEAN-AFRICAN-MIDDLE EASTERN CAMPAIGN MEDAL	36	COMBAT MEDICAL BADGE
11	AIR MEDAL	24	WW II VICTORY MEDAL	37	EXPERT FIELD MEDICAL BADGE
12	JOINT SERVICE COMMENDATION MEDAL	25	ARMY OF OCCUPATION MEDAL	38	LETTER "V" DEVICE
13	ARMY COMMENDATION MEDAL	26	MEDAL FOR HUMANE ACTION	39	OAK LEAF CLUSTER

40	SERVICE STAR
41	BRONZE ARROWHEAD
42	FRENCH FOURRAGERE
43	BELGIAN FOURRAGERE
44	NETHERLANDS ORANGE LANYARD
45	PHILIPPINE DEFENSE RIBBON
46	PHILIPPINE LIBERATION RIBBON
47	PHILIPPINE INDEPENDENCE RIBBON
48	UNITED NATIONS SERVICE MEDAL
49	REPUBLIC OF VIETNAM CAMPAIGN RIBBON W/DEVICE (1960)
50	
51	
52	

The Secretary of the Army directs that the following awards be engraved according to current regulations and issued to address shown below. (Engraving to be as indicated in classification or below.)

AWARD CODE	STARS BRONZE	STARS SILVER	OAK LEAF CLUSTERS BRONZE	OAK LEAF CLUSTERS SILVER	ARROW-HEAD	CLASP	GOLD STAR LAPEL BUTTON ENGRAVE	ISSUE	TYPE
9								☐ COST ☐ GRATUITOUSLY	☐ CLUTCH ☐ PIN
14									
15									
23	1								
24									
34									
Honorable Service Lapel Button WWII									
//////NOTHING FOLLOWS//////									

REMARKS   Your medals will be shipped to you by the Commander, U.S. Army Support Command, USA Support Activity, Attention: STRAP-SEI, P. O. Box 13460, Philadelphia, Pennsylvania 19101-3460, within approximately 30 to 45 days from the date of the DA Form 1577.

The Bronze Star Medal is based on the award of the Combat Infantryman Badge.

Appropriately inscribed certificate(s) enclosed.

US ARMY SUPPORT CENTER
PHILADELPHIA, PENNSYLVANIA 19101
OFFICIAL BUSINESS
PENALTY FOR PRIVATE USE, $300

POSTAGE AND FEES PAID
DEPARTMENT OF THE ARMY
DOD - 314

J. C. HERBERT
LTC, U.S. Army
Adjutant General

DA FORM 1577
1 NOV 73   REPLACES EDITION OF 1 JUL 66, WHICH WILL BE USED.

Image source: Neal Abbott per National Archives and Records Administration

Sources:

32. Utah State Archives and Records Service; Salt Lake City, Utah; Military Service Cards, ca. 1898-1975; Creating Agency: Department of Administrative Services, Division of Archives and Records Service; Series: 85268; Reel: 49, viewed 14 February 2019, accessed 14 February 2019

33. Federal Security Agency, United States Public Health Service, National Office of Vital Statistics, State of Utah Certificate of Death, Registrar #4, accessed 15 February 2019

34. Abbott, Dale Cary, "Details of Samuel Bennett Abbott's Military Service," Interview by Kathleen Mays, Military Service of the Abbotts, 16 February 2019

35. Abbott, Neal Alan, "Details of Samuel Bennett Abbott's Military Service," Interview by Kathleen Mays, Military Service of the Abbotts, 16 February 2019

36. Wikipedia, The Free Encyclopedia, National Personnel Records Center fire, https://en.wikipedia.org/wiki/National_Personnel_Records_Center_fire, accessed 28 Apr 2019

37. Primary-National Personnel Records Centers, Military Personnel Records, 9700 Page Boulevard, St. Louis, Missouri 63132-5100, NA Form 13045 (Rev 9-90), Secondary-Neal Alan Abbott on behalf of the Abbott family, Tertiary-Kathleen C. Abbott Mays, received 8 Mar 2019 via USPS, digitally scanned 9 Mar 2019

Elisha W Franklin

1st Sergeant · United States Army · Served 1898
Of the Abbott / Cary line

Front Left to Right: Merle Forest, Elisha W Franklin, Hazel Mirth Franklin, Volney Franklin, Agnes Franklin, Flora Ann Barnaby Franklin, Horace Greeley Franklin
Back Left to Right: Edna Lucy Forest, Thomas Paine Franklin, Benjamin Franklin, John Franklin, Estella Franklin, Edith Victoria Franklin

Elisha W. Franklin was born on the 4th of May, 1850 to John and Lucy Carter Franklin in Lenawee, Lenawee Co., Michigan. He was the 7th of 8 children born to John and Lucy.

Elisha married Flora Ann Barnaby on the 6th of April, 1877. They

Image source: Schmelding, Allen Bartell

69

Image source: Allen Bartell

April 28, to May 7, 1898 (both dates inclusive)
Mustered-in U. S. Service May 8, 1898.

REPORT OF ADJUTANT GENERAL.   89

Fourteenth Regiment—Continued.

COMPANY K.

Name.	Rank.	Age	Nativity.	Residence.
Elisha B. Wood	Captain	51	Indiana	Long Prairie, Minn.
Irving A. Caswell	1st Lieutenant	28	Minnesota	Arcka, Minn.
William C. Smiley	2nd Lieutenant	26	Pennsylvania	St. Paul, Minn.
Elisha W. Franklin	Sergeant	35	Michigan	Staples, Minn.
Arthur J. Woodin	Sergeant	30	Minnesota	Park Rapids, Minn.
Hal B. Thompson	Sergeant	24	Kansas	Holton, Kan.
Clide P. Mattison	Sergeant	21	Minnesota	Long Prairie, Minn.
Leroy McNeice	Sergeant	21	Minnesota	Sauk Centre, Minn.
David H. Mott	Sergeant	27	Minnesota	Akley, Minn.
John T. Jones	Corporal	21	Minnesota	Long Prairie, Minn.

Elisha W. Franklin ✓	Sergeant	35

had 11 children; Edna Lucy, Edith Victoria, Estella, Benjamin, John, Thomas Payne, Horace G, Volney, Hazel Mirth, Agnes, and Luther Elisha.

It has been suggested that he served in the Civil War, although I can only find evidence of his service from 1877 to 1886 and in the Spanish American War in 1898 in the 14th Regiment, Minnesota Infantry, K Company as a 1st Sergeant.

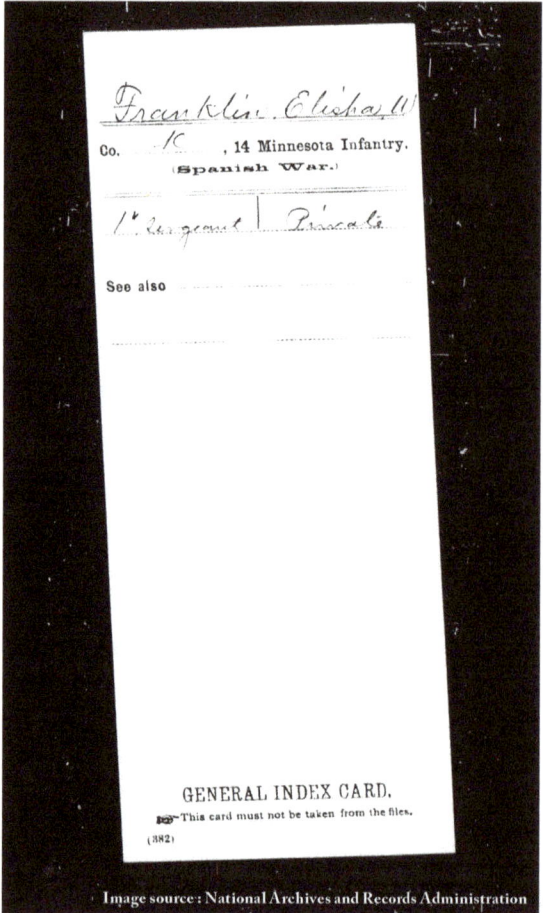

Franklin. Elisha, W

Co. K , 14 Minnesota Infantry.
(Spanish War.)

1st Sergeant | Private

See also

GENERAL INDEX CARD.
This card must not be taken from the files.
(3382)

Image source: National Archives and Records Administration

Image source : National Archives and Records Administration

Elisha died on the 3rd of January, 1917 at Rush, Elbert, Colorado and is buried in the Kanza Cemetery near there.

Sources:

38. United States Index to Service Records, War with Spain, 1898," database with images, FamilySearch (https://familysearch.org/ark:/61903/3:1:33SQ-GTRM-9LBG?cc=1919583&wc=3K4C-3TG%3A211565701 : 22 May 2014), Fom-Fran > image 2233

of 2400; citing NARA microfilm publication M871 (Washington D.C.: National Archives and Records Administration, n.d.), accessed 1 Mar 2019

39. U.S. Returns from Regular Army Infantry Regiments, 1821-1916 for Elisha W Franklin, accessed 2 Mar 2019

40. U.S., Spanish American War Volunteers Index to Compiled Military Service Records, 1898 for Elisha W Franklin, accessed 2 Mar 2019

41. FamilySearch, EW Franklin 14th Reg Co K, accessed 26 Feb 2019

Riley Garner Clark

Private · United States Army · Served 1846-1848

Of the Philpott / Bringard line

Riley Garner Clark was born on the 29th of July, 1829 to Samuel & Rebecca Garner Clark in Marion, Clinton Co., Ohio. He was the 2nd of 13 children.

He enlisted in the United States Army, along with his brother Joseph, on the 16th of July, 1846 at Council Bluffs, Iowa along with approximately 500 Mormon volunteers at the request of President Brigham Young, the Prophet of The Church of Jesus Christ of Latter Day Saints. He was assigned to Captain Jefferson Hunt, The Iowa Mormon Battalion, Company A under command of General Kearney.

The Mormon Battalion, the only religion-based unit in United States military history, served from July 1846 – July 1847 during the Mexican–American War of 1846–1848. The battalion was a volunteer unit of between 534 and 559 Latter-day Saint men, led by Mormon company officers commanded by regular U.S. Army officers. During its service, the

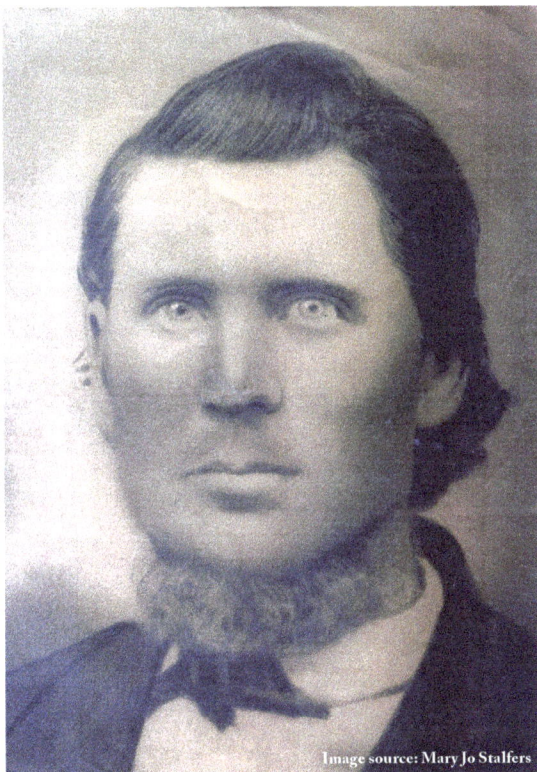

Image source: Mary Jo Stalfers

battalion made a grueling march of nearly 2,000 miles from Council Bluffs, Iowa, to San Diego, California.

Excerpt from Biography of Riley Garner Clark by Ada Clark Carter:

President Brigham Young promised the Mormon boys who enlisted in the army if they would be faithful to their God they would not be required to fight, which promise was fulfilled.

While on their march to San Diego they endured many hardships. At one time, both men and teams had marched all day without water. When the last of their provisions were gone, beefs were killed, this being their only food.

The battalion boys experienced much suffering due to exposure. Many were poorly clad and destitute of tents and wagon covers. Sickness

Image source: BYU Center For Family History

was prevalent in the camps and many of them died, but they never wavered in their purpose.

A song "The Lonesome Howling wolves," was composed by one of the group and sung over the graves of those that had died. The chorus was as follows:

We burnt ashes and coal over the graves,
To hide him from the savages,
And the lonesome howling wolves.

Father used to sing this to his children. While singing the chorus he used the carpenter saw, by running his fingers up the blade, to demonstrate the howling of the wolves. Father sang the chorus of another song:

How hard to starve us out,
Upon this sandy desert route.

After a long and perilous journey the battalion arrived in California, January 29, 1847. Their camps were located a mile below the Catholic Mission and some four or more miles from the seaport town of San Diego.

The battalion served one year in San Diego. While there, the men were permitted to visit many places of interest. Among them were the old mission home at San Diego, the old San Gabriel mission at Los Angeles and other places of interest.

After serving, the men were honorably released at San Diego. General Kearney was more than pleased with his Mormon boys. He lifted his hat with martial pride and said, "Over the Alps Napoleon went, but these men crossed the whole continent."

Return list of Mormon Battalion Company A.

Image source: BYU Library Digital Collections

It was the greatest march of infantry in the history of the world. Their return trip was made by way of the southern route. Here again they endured many hardships. While crossing the desert they suffered from the heat and want of water. Their tongues became dry, parched and swollen. They happily welcomed a rain, as they would run to the puddles of water, lie down, and drink to quench their burning thirst. Their feet became sore and bleeding that made it very difficult to travel.

Extreme thirst threatened their health and survival. Battalion member Henry G. Boyle said, "We were all weary and

Military Service in the Abbott Family

fatigued, hungry, nearly naked, and barefoot, but our burning thirst drowned every other suffering."

Many went to great lengths to quench their thirst by using quills to suck water through cracks in rocks and by putting stones or buckshot in their mouths to generate moisture. On at least one occasion, they drank water from mud holes, lying down and "lap[ping] it like a dog." After one waterless stretch on the march, Colonel Philip St. George Cooke observed, "Any other company under like circumstances would have mutinized."

Note: Some have called the Mormon Battalion's journey the longest overland march in military history, but this notion is false.

Riley Garner Clark Headstone

Historian Sherman L. Fleek provides several examples of marches that exceeded in distance the Mormon Battalion's march. See Fleek, History May Be Searched in Vain: A Military History of the Mormon Battalion (Spokane: Arthur H. Clark Company, 2006), 324–27.

Riley Garner Clark died on the 11th of July, 1876 at Panguitch, Garfield Co., Utah, USA

Sources:

42. Weltha Clark Bringard Genealogical Records, accessed 13 May 1991

43. Biography of Riley Garner Clark by Ada Clark Carter, FamilySearch, https://www.familysearch.org/photos/artifacts/10498417, accessed 7 Mar 2019

44. Wikipedia, Mormon Battalion, https://en.m.wikipedia.org/wiki/Mormon_Battalion, (1) Fleek 2006, (2) Black, Susan Easton (1994), Powell, Allen Kent, ed., Utah History Encyclopedia, Salt Lake City, Utah: University of Utah Press, archived from the original on April 11, 2013, (3) "Historic Events", CaliforniaPioneer.org, California Pioneer Heritage Foundation, retrieved April 9, 2013, (4) Lloyd, R. Scott (June 6, 1992), "Monument honoring Mormon Battalion to regain its luster", Church News, accessed 17 Mar 2019

45. Four Things to Know about the Journey of the Mormon Battalion by Brandon J. Metcalf, 21 March 2019, https://history.churchofjesuschrist.org/content/historic-sites/journey-of-the-mormon-battalion?lang=eng, accessed 17 Mar 2019

46. The Mormon Battalion Association, Soldiers in the Mormon Battalion, Alphabetical List of Soldiers, https://mormonbattalion.com/alphabetical-list-of-battalion-soldiers/, accessed 17 Mar 2019

47. Henry G. Boyle journal, Jan. 16, 1847, in Autobiography and Diary of Henry G. Boyle, 1832–1855, typescript, Church History Library, Salt Lake City; punctuation and capitalization standardized., https://history.lds.org/article/historic-sites/journey-of-the-mormon-battalion?lang=eng, accessed 17 Mar 2019

48. Hyde, The Private Journal of William Hyde, 35–36., https://history.lds.org/article/historic-sites/journey-of-the-mormon-battalion?lang=eng, accessed 17 Mar 2019

John William Philpot

Captain · Confederate States Army
Served 1861-1865
Of the Philpott / Bringard line

John William Philpott was born in 1821 to William and Elizabeth Walker Philpott In North Carolina. He enlisted in the Confederate States Army on the 25th of September, 1861.

Image source: Caleb Strausbaugh, FamilySearch

He was in Company E of the 35th Regiment, North Carolina Infantry, ranking in as a Corporal. The 35th Regiment, North Carolina Infantry was organized on November 8, 1861, at Camp Mangum, near Raleigh, North Carolina.

Its members were raised in the counties of Mecklenburg, Onslow, McDowell, Moore, Chatham, Person, Union, Henderson, Wayne, and Catawba. Available statistics for total numbers of men listed as:

- Enlisted or commissioned: 1506
- Drafted: 13
- Transferred in: 42
- Killed or died of wounds: 122
- Died of disease: 233
- Prisoner of war: 456
- Died while prisoner of war: 33
- Disabled: 61
- Missing: 4
- Deserted: 34
- Discharged: 95
- Transferred out: 40

After fighting at New Bern, the regiment was ordered to Virginia and assigned to General R. Ransom's and M.W.

© Kathleen C. Mays

Ransom's Brigade. It participated in the difficult campaigns of the Army of Northern Virginia from the Seven Days' Battles to Fredericksburg.

Ordered back to North Carolina, it fought at Boon's Mill and Plymouth, then returned to Virginia in May, 1864. The 35th saw action at Drewry's Bluff, endured the hardships of the Petersburg siege south of the James River, and ended the war at Appomattox.

This unit sustained 127 casualties at Malvern Hill, 25 in the Maryland Campaign, 29 at Fredericksburg, and 103 at Plymouth. Many were disabled at Saylor's Creek, and on April 9, 1865, it surrendered 5 officers and 111 men at Appomattox Court House, Virginia, 5 officers and 111 men, with John William's rank as a Captain,.

The field officers were Colonels James T. Johnson, John G. Jones, Matthew W. Ransom, and James Sinclair; Lieutenant Colonels M.D. Craton, Oliver C. Petway, and Simon B. Taylor; and Majors John M. Kelly and Robert E. Petty.

John William Philpot died in 1892 at Durham Township, Orange Co., North Carolina, USA.

Sources:

49. JW Philpot Enlist Info U.S., Confederate Soldiers Compiled Service Records, 1861-1865 - Ancestry.com, accessed 1 Mar 2019

50. John W Philpott U.S. Civil War Soldiers, 1861-1865 - Ancestry.com, https://search.ancestry.com/cgi-bin/sse.dll?_phsrc=Sea127&_phstart=successSource&usePUBJs=true&indiv=1&db=civilwar_histdatasys&gsfn=John%20W&gsln=Philpot&gsln_x=NP_NN_NS&msrpn__ftp=north%20carolina,%20usa&msrpn=36&msipn__ftp=north%20carolina,%20usa&msipn=36&new=1&rank=1&redir=false&uidh=2xb&gss=angs-d&pcat=39&fh=0&h=2999925&recoff=&ml_rpos=1, Historical Data Systems, comp. U.S., Civil War Soldier Records and Profiles, 1861-1865 [database on-line]. Provo, UT, USA: Ancestry.com Operations Inc, 2009., Original data: Data compiled by Historical Data Systems of Kingston, MA, Historical Data Systems, Inc., PO Box 35. Duxbury, MA 02331., accessed 2 Mar 2019

51. Thomas Legion 35th North Carolina Infantry Regiment: Battles and Casualties, http://www.thomaslegion.net/35thnorthcarolinainfantryregimentbattlesandcasualties.html information obtained through: Confederate Military History, Extended Edition (19 Volumes); The Union Army (9 Volumes); Walter Clark, Histories of the Several Regiments and Battalions From North Carolina in the Great War 1861-1865 (5 Volumes); North Carolina Troops 1861-1865: A Roster (15 Volumes); Official Records of the Union and Confederate Armies, accessed 5 Mar 2019

52. National Park Service, The Civil War, Battle Unit Details, Confederate North Carolina Troops, 35th Regiment, North Carolina Infantry, Overview, https://www.nps.gov/civilwar/search-battle-units-detail.htm?battleUnitCode=CNC0035RI viewed, accessed, 3/5/2019

53. 35th Regiment North Carolina Infantry,and Family Search https://familysearch.org/wiki/en/35th_Regiment,_North_Carolina_Infantry, accessed 5 March 2019

Frederick William Christoph Fuhrmeister

Musketier · Royal Prussian Army
Served 1839-1842
Of the Abbott / Cary line

Image source: Leah Whipple, FamilySearch

Image source: Lea Giberson, FamilySearch

Frederick William Christoph Fuhrmeister, Americanized surname of Foremaster, was born on the 2nd of January, 1821 to Heinrich Andreas and Maria Catherina Dorothea Landes Fuhrmeister in Dardesheim, Halberstadt, Saxony, Prussia, later known as Germany.

He was the 8th child of 14 children born to this union. Frederick married Christina Sophia Magdalena Lindau on the 24th of August, 1844 at Deersheim, Halberstadt, Saxony, Prussia. This Union was blessed with 12 children.

At that time, in Prussia, all males that turned 18 years of age were compelled to serve in the King's army for three years. After his discharge three years later, he returned to Dardesheim but was subject to recall at any time if the country was threatened with war.

Fredrick died on the 4th of July, 1892 at Fredonia, Cocino, Arizona, USA

Image source: Lea Giberson, FamilySearch

Sources:

54. FamilySearch Family Tree, online database, https://www.familysearch.org/tree/person/details/ KWJC-YTX, accessed 26 February 2019

55. Life and History of Frederick William Foremaster, 1821-1892, Written by his granddaughter Florence Foremaster, St. George, Utah, April 1977, https://www.familysearch.org/photos/ artifacts/2005100?p=18813383&returnLabel=Friedrick%20William%20Christoph%20 Fuhrmeister%20(KWJC-YTX)&returnUrl=https%3A%2F%2Fwww.familysearch.org%2Ftree% 2Fperson%2Fmemories%2FKWJC-YTX, accessed 26 February 2019

Alvin Pope Barnaby

Private · United States Army · Served 1864 - 1865
Of the Abbott / Cary line

Alvin Pope Barnaby was born on the 17th of October, 1821 to Alvin Perry and Minerva Markham Barnaby in Sandusky, Erie Co., Ohio, US.

His father moved his family from Ohio to Michigan and settled in Cass County in 1825. Here Alvin lived and developed into manhood, receiving the advantage afforded by

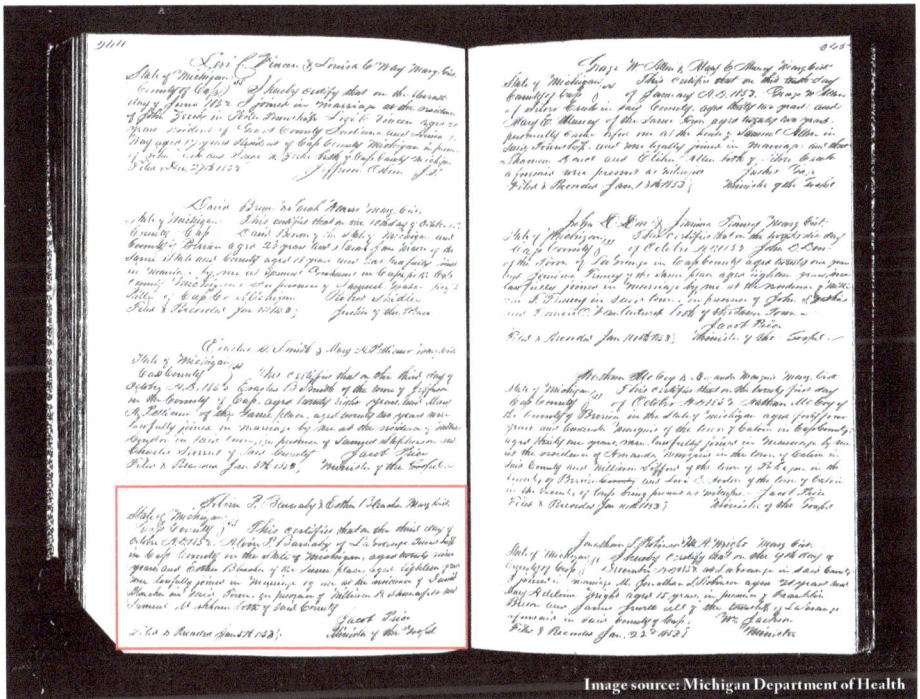

Marriage record of Alvin Barnaby and Esther Bleacher.

Image source: Michigan Department of Health

the common schools of the county. Mr. Barnaby was married October 3, 1853, to Miss Esther, daughter of Daniel and Mary Barr Bleacher.

Name:	Alvan P Barnaby
Enlistment Age:	42
Birth Date:	1821
Enlistment Date:	23 Jan 1864
Enlistment Place:	Dowagiac, Michigan
Enlistment Rank:	Private
Muster Date:	26 Jan 1864
Muster Place:	Michigan
Muster Company:	M
Muster Regiment:	1st Cavalry
Muster Regiment Type:	Cavalry
Muster Information:	Enlisted
Casualty Date:	18 Aug 1864
Casualty Place:	Philadelphia, Pennsylvania
Type of Casualty:	Hospitalized
Casualty Information:	Satterlee Hospital, sick with measles
Muster Out Date:	24 May 1865
Muster Out Place:	Philadelphia, Pennsylvania
Muster Out Information:	disch disability
Side of War:	Union
Survived War?:	Yes
Residence Place:	Volinia, Michigan
Last Known Residence Place:	Gratiot County, Michigan
Death Date:	13 May 1881
Burial Place:	North Star, Gratiot Co., Michigan
Cemetery Plot Number:	43
Notes:	1865-01-26 Furloughed, (Philadelphia, PA), Satterlee Hospital
Additional Notes 2:	Casualty 2 Date: 25 Feb 1865; Casualty 2 Place: Philadelphia, Pennsylvania; Casualty 2 Casualty Type: Hospitalized; Casualty 2 Information: Satterlee Hospital;
Title:	Record of Service of Michigan Volunteers 1861-65; The Medical and Surgical History of the Civil War; SUVCW Database: http://www.suvcwdb.org/

He enlisted at Doagiac, Cass County, Michigan on January 23, 1864 in the United States Army. Alvin was a Private in Civil War M Company, 1st Calvary Regiment, Michigan.

At the time of his enlistment, he was living in Volinia Township, Cass County, Michigan with his wife, Esther, and four of the ten children born to them.

Private Barnaby was stricken with disease a few days before his regiment fought in the "Battle of the Wilderness" and he did not convalesce until after the war.

On the 9th of April, 1865, his regiment was involved in the battle at Appomattox Court House, Virginia, one of the last battles fought to end this terrible conflict.

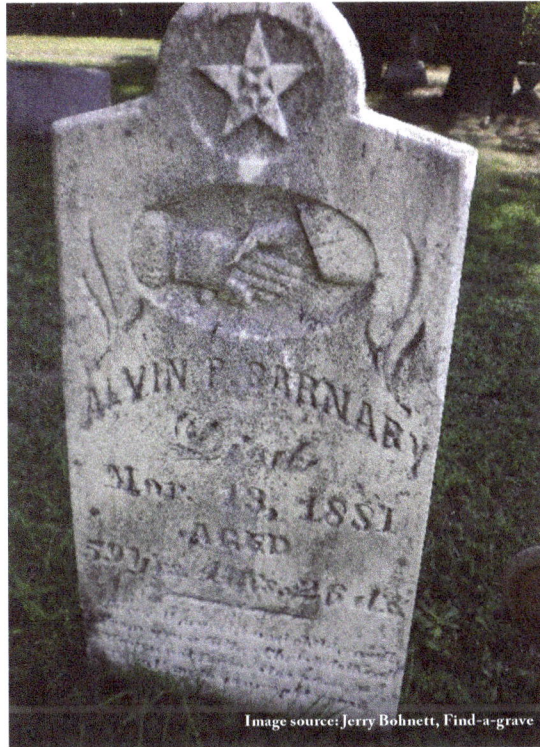

Image source: Jerry Bohnett, Find-a-grave

He was honorably discharged at Philadelphia, Pennsylvania on May 24, 1865, having served for 15 months. After returning home to Cass County, he continued in the carpenter's trade, which he was accomplished at.

Alvin and Esther were blessed with ten children, Daniel, Mary A, Francis E, Flora A, Ezra A, Ulyses S, Perry I, James H, Bertha M, and Daniel V, nine of whom lived until adulthood.

Alvin died on the 13th of March, 1881 at North Star, Gratiot, Michigan, United States. Inscribed on his headstone is the following, "Farewell my wife and children all, from you a father Christ shall call. Mourn not for me it is in vain, to call me to your sight again."

Sources:

56. FamilySearch.org, Alvin Pope Barnaby, Memories, https://www.familysearch.org/tree/person/LW9W-CB5, accessed 23 March 2023

57. Find a Grave, database and images (https://www.findagrave.com/memorial/17470928/alvin-pope-barnaby: accessed 20 April 2023), memorial page for Alvin Pope Barnaby (18 Oct 1821–13 Mar 1881), Find a Grave Memorial ID 17470928, citing North Star Cemetery, North Star, Gratiot County, Michigan, USA; Maintained by Glenn Geirland (contributor 40342511).

Stephen Straughn
Private · Continental Army · Served 1781
Of the Philpott / Bringard line

Stephen Straughan, also spelled Strawn or Stron, was born in 1757 at Caroline, Virginia, British Colonial America to Richard and Lucy Poe Straughan. Stephen was the 2nd of 9 children.

He served as a Private in the Chatham County Regiment, under North Carolina's Captain Alexander Clark in 1781. Without stating why, Stephen's brother, Richard, reports that he filled in for the final two months of Stephen's enlistment.

Stephen Straughan married Frances Ferguson in Chatham, North Carolina in the year 1777 and died sometime after 1805, also in Chatham, North Carolina.

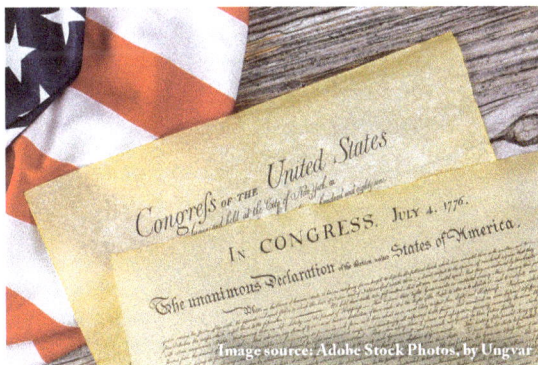

Image source: Adobe Stock Photos, by Ungvar

Sources:

58. Daughters of the American Revolution, Genealogy Research, DAR Ancestor #: A111248, See: https://services.dar.org/Public/DAR_Research/search_adb/?action=full&p_id=A111248, accessed 29 March 2023

59. The American Revolution in North Carolina, The Patriots and Their Forces, The Privates, Horsemen, Fifers, Drummers, etc. - Last Names Beginning with "S", https://www.carolana.com/NC/Revolution/nc_patriot_military_privates_s.html, accessed 30 March 2023

Military Service in the Abbott Family

James Abbott

Sergeant · Continental Army, Connecticut Line
Served 1776 - 1777

Of the Abbott / Cary line

Headstone of James Abbott.

James Abbott was born on the 9th of March, 1753 to Abiel and Abigail Fenton Abbott in Hampton, Windham, Connecticut Colony, British Colonial America.

He served in Captain Clark's Co., Col Sage's Regiment, Sage's Regiment, 1776–77, during the Revolutionary War in the Connecticut Line.

Gravesite of James Abbott.

His father, Abiel, was a grantee in the Susquehana Purchase of 1754. James acquired half of the lots until he sold them to Matthias Hollenback on June 13, 1787.

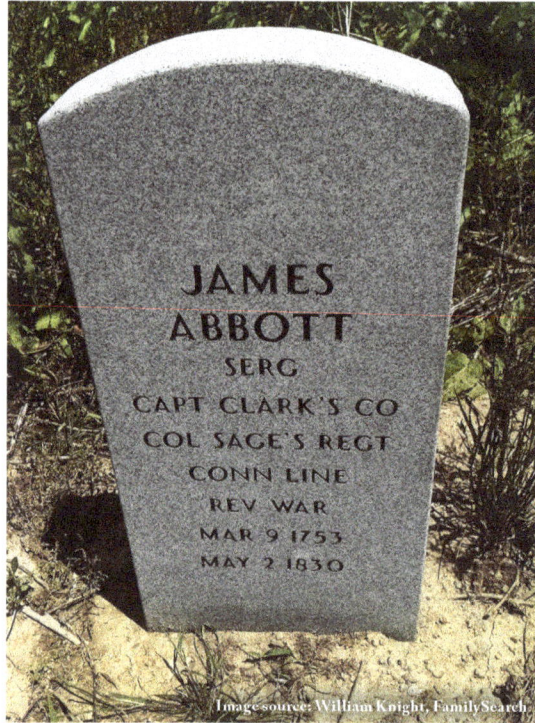

Memorial of Sgt. James Abbott.

James and his wife Phoebe operated a linen weaving mill. He moved from Wyoming Valley, Pennsylvania, the site of the Wyoming Massacre of July 3, 1778, to the Canisteo Valley, New York and settled near Arkport about 1806.

His tombstone bears the following inscription: "To the Memory of James Abbott, one of the patriots of 1776, who died May 2, 1830. Aged 77 years." He died in Hornell, Steuben, New York, US.

Sources:

60. FamilySearch.org, Family Tree online database, James Abbott, https://www.familysearch.org/tree/person/L635-X92, accessed 21 March 2023

61. American Revolutionary War, Connecticut Regiments in the Continental Army, https://revolutionarywar.us/continental-army/connecticut/, accessed 22 March 2023

The United States of America

honors the memory of

James Abbott

This certificate is awarded by a grateful nation in recognition of devoted and selfless consecration to the service of our country in the Armed Forces of the United States.

President of the United States

Stephen Harding
Captain · Pennsylvania Militia · About 1776 - 1778
Of the Abbott / Cary line

Stephen Harding was born on the 13th of January, 1749 to Stephen Jr. and Amelia Amy Gardiner Harding in Colchester, Hartford, Connecticut Colony, British Colonial America. He was the 4th child of 14 children.

Stephen came to the Wyoming Valley, PA in 1772. He became one of the Proprietors of Exeter when that town was erected in 1772 and settled there in 1774. Stephen may have been in the party attacked by Indians shortly before the Wyoming Massacre in July 1778. If so, he escaped into the woods and returned to Jenkins Fort that night.

Image source: N. J. P. McClure, Ancestry

Above: Headstone
Below: Revolutionary Plaque

He enlisted and served as private in Captain Robert Durkee's Company, the First Westmoreland Independent Company, in the War of the American Revolution. He later served as a Captain in the Pennsylvania Militia and settled in Exeter, Pennsylvania.

He married Prudence Jane Gustin between 1762 to 1765 and they were

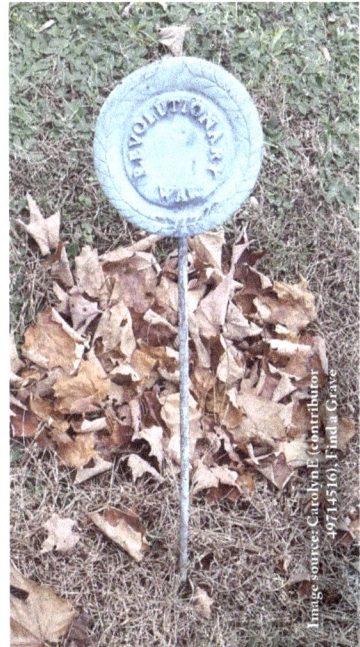

Image source: Carolyn E (contributor 49714516), Find a Grave

Image source: Pennsylvania Probate Records, 1683-1994

blessed with 7 daughters and 1 son. Stephen died on the 4th of August, 1816 and was probably the first person buried in the historic Harding Cemetery in Exeter.

Sources:

62. Find a Grave, database and images (https://www.findagrave.com/memorial/41636728/stephen-harding: accessed 29 March 2023), memorial page for Capt Stephen Harding (13 Jan 1749–10 Aug 1816), Find a Grave Memorial ID 41636728, citing Harding Cemetery, Exeter, Luzerne County, Pennsylvania, USA; Maintained by CarolynE (contributor 49714516). Accessed 29 March 2023

63. "Pennsylvania Cemetery Records, ca. 1700-ca. 1950," database, FamilySearch (https://familysearch.org/ark:/61903/3:1:3QS7-L983-4QSR?cc=3743478 : 4 July 2020), > image 1 of 1; Church of Jesus Christ of Latter-day Saints. Family History Department., accessed 29 March 2023

64. Blair, Williams T. (1924). The Michael Shoemaker Book. International Press, Scranton, PA., Page 513

65. Brittanica, Wyoming Massacre, United States History, Written and fact-checked by The Editors of Encyclopaedia Britannica, https://www.britannica.com/event/Wyoming-Massacre, accessed 30 March 2023

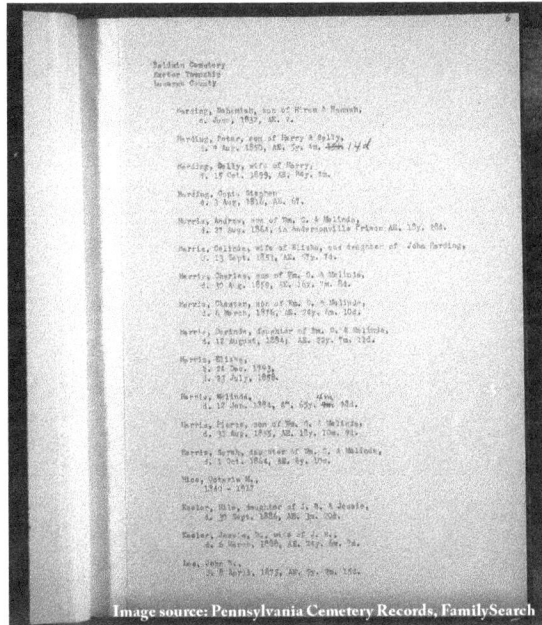

Image source: Pennsylvania Cemetery Records, FamilySearch

Stephen Harding

97

Military Service in the Abbott Family

John Franklin Jr.

Colonel · American Patriots & Loyalists
Served 1775-1780
Of the Abbott / Cary line

John Franklin Jr. was born on the 15th of September, 1749 to John and Keziah Pierce Franklin in Canaan, Litchfield Co., Colony of Connecticut, British Colonial America.

He fought for the Independence of America, celebrated in the Yankee and Pennant struggles, had for his associates the brave men who settled Sheshequin, Bradford County, Pennsylvania.

When the 24th regiment of Connecticut Militia was organized in 1775, he was made captain of the Salem and Huntington Company. At the battle of Wyoming, Franklin and his company were directed to report at Forty Fort immediately, but his company was so scattered that he was unable to bring them on in time to participate in the battle.

John Franklin

Image source: Jennifer Lynn Middleton, FamilySearch

Of himself, he says, as soon as he had taken care of his family, he set out with what few of his company could be gathered for

Wyoming, and reached the fort too late to participate in the engagement. He was present, however, to lend his advice in regard to the surrender and his aid to the fugitives.

The Battle of Wyoming (also known as the Wyoming Massacre) was an encounter during the American Revolutionary War between American Patriots and Loyalists accompanied by Iroquois raiders that took place in the Wyoming Valley of Pennsylvania on July 3, 1778. More than three hundred Patriots were killed in the battle.

John Franklin's Home, West View, by Stanley Jones, April 12, 1937.

Those who had returned to Wyoming for better protection had formed themselves into a military company, of which he was made the captain; he was also appointed a justice of the peace, so that he combined in himself both the highest military and civil functions in Wyoming, and to his decisions all bowed with respect and confidence.

Military Service in the Abbott Family

In the expedition of Colonel Hartley, in the autumn of 1778, were two companies from Wyoming; 58 men of the Independent company under Captain Simon Spalding, and 12 volunteers of the Militia Company commanded by Franklin.

In this expedition, Franklin and his men were in the forefront and won the greatest praise of their commander. In Sullivan's campaign he was captain of the Wyoming Volunteers, and in the attack of General Hand on Chemung, known as Hogback Hill, he was severely wounded in the shoulder, which, of course, prevented further participation in the campaign.

From the return of this expedition in October of 1779 until the close of the war, scouting parties of the Wyoming Militia were out daily. It was imperative that they watch exposed points, pursue marauding bands of Tories and Indians, and protect workmen on their farms. These tasks were a service that required the utmost skill and judgment of the commandant.

John died on the 1st of March, 1831 at Athens Township, Bradford Co., Pennsylvania, USA.

Sources:

66. Find A Grave, database and images (https://www.findagrave.com : accessed 02 March 2019), memorial page for Col John Franklin (15 Sep 1749–1 Mar 1831), Find A Grave Memorial no. 43432551, citing Franklin-Flower Cemetery, Athens, Bradford County, Pennsylvania, USA ; Maintained by LDR (contributor 47171969), accessed 18 February 2019

67. Wikipedia, The Free Encyclopedia, Battle of Wyoming, https://en.m.wikipedia.org/wiki/Battle_of_Wyoming, viewed, accessed 19 February 2019

Military Service in the Abbott Family

Wait Bradford, also spelled as Waite Bradford, was born on the 20th of June, 1732 to Ephraim and Elizabeth Brewster Bradford in Kingston, Plymouth, British Colonial America.

Wait, a great-grandson of Governor William Bradford, married Wealtha Bassett on the 1st of November, 1765 in Kingston, Plymouth, Massachusetts. Their Union was blessed with two daughters and two sons; Sarah, Simeon, Deborah, and Ephraim.

He was a resident of Pembroke, Plymouth, Massachusetts when he enlisted in the Massachusetts Militia on the 25th of June, 1776 and served in Captain William Weston's Company. He was stationed at the Gurnet for defense of Plymouth harbor during the Revolutionary War.

Wait was discharged on 19 Nov 1776 and according to the "History of Turner, Maine From Its Settlement To 1886," Wait and Welthea, also spelled as Wealtha, resided in Duxbury,

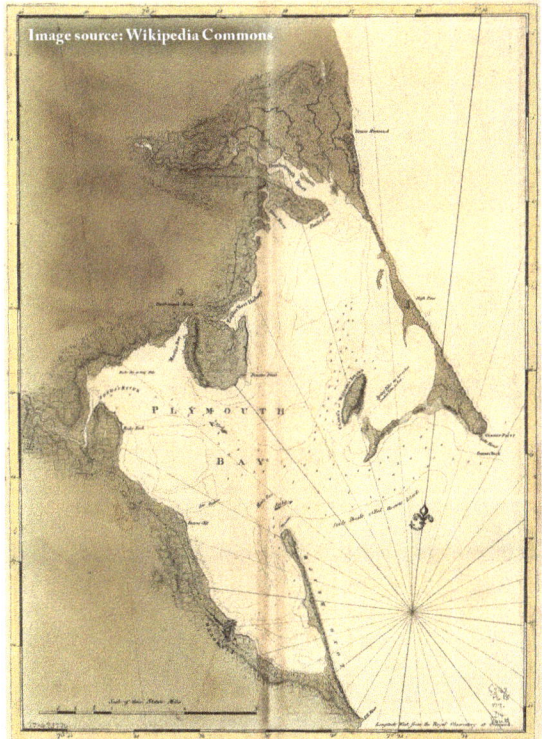

Image source: Wikipedia Commons

Chart of Plymouth Bay.

Plymouth, Massachusetts from January of 1779 to December of 1779. In 1792, they moved to Turner, Oxford, Maine, which was originally called Sylvester, Canada in 1690.

Wait died on the 20th of October, 1801 at Turner, Androscoggin, Maine, USA.

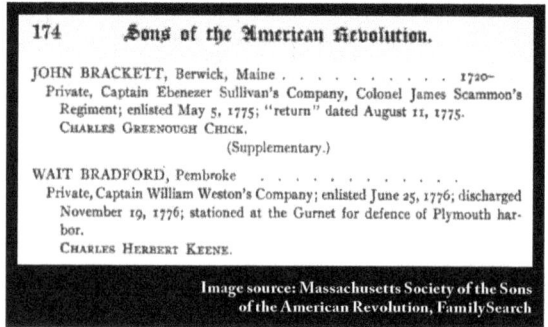

174　　Sons of the American Revolution.

JOHN BRACKETT, Berwick, Maine 1720–
　　Private, Captain Ebenezer Sullivan's Company, Colonel James Scammon's Regiment; enlisted May 5, 1775; "return" dated August 11, 1775.
　　CHARLES GREENOUGH CHICK.
　　　　　　　(Supplementary.)

WAIT BRADFORD, Pembroke . . . .
　　Private, Captain William Weston's Company; enlisted June 25, 1776; discharged November 19, 1776; stationed at the Gurnet for defence of Plymouth harbor.
　　CHARLES HERBERT KEENE.

Image source: Massachusetts Society of the Sons of the American Revolution, FamilySearch

Sources:

68. FamilySearch.org, Family Tree online database, Wait Bradford, https://www.familysearch.org/tree/person/LZGQ-KV3, Memories, accessed 24 March, 2023

69. Bent, Samuel Arthur, Massachusetts Society of the Sons of the American Revolution, Register for 1904 with lists of members and their Revolutionary ancestors, p. 174, accessed 24 March 2023

70. Massachusetts, Office of the Secretary of State, Massachusetts Soldiers And Sailors Of The War Of The Revolution, a compilation from the archives, Volume 2, p. 408, Volumes published from 1896 to 1908

Abiel Abbott

Captain · Connecticut Militia · Served Before 1772
Of the Abbott / Cary line

Abiel Abbott was born on the 3rd of March, 1726 to Phillip & Abigail Bickford Abbott in Windham Twp, Windham, Connecticut, British Colonial America.

According to "A Genealogical Record of George Abbot and His Descendents," Abiel was "much respected for his good sense, moral, and religious character, and usefulness."

Abiel was married at Windham, June 5, 1750 to Abigail Fenton. According to Find-a-Grave, there were five children born to Abiel and Abigail, yet the Family Tree on

Image source: William Knight, FamilySearch

FamilySearch.org lists the following six children: Phillip Abbott, 1751-1834; James Abbott, 1753-1830; Abiel Abbott Jr., 1754-1830; Abigail Abbott, 1763-1838; Amelia Abbott, 1763-1843; and Anna Abbott, 1765-1846.

Abiel Abbott was a captain in the Connecticut militia, and a farmer. He was named as one of the grantees in the Indian Deed of July 1754.

Abiel died May 21, 1772 at Windham, He was found dead in his field, "supposed to have died of a fit." The inscription on his gravestone is:

"In Memory of Cap Abiel Abbott the beloved consort of Abigail who departed this life May 22, 1772"

Sources:

71. FamilySearch.org, Family Tree online database, Captain Abiel Abbott, https://www.familysearch.org/tree/person/L8ZZ-YX1, accessed 21 March 2023

72. Find a Grave, database and images (https://www.findagrave.com/memorial/79973459/abiel-abbott: accessed 21 March 2023), memorial page for Capt Abiel Abbott (3 Mar 1726–22 May 1772), Find a Grave Memorial ID 79973459, citing North Cemetery, Hampton, Windham County, Connecticut, USA; Maintained by John Beckstein (contributor 46939506).

73. History of Wilkes-Barre, Lucerne County, Pennsylvania, From Its First Beginnings To The Present Time; Including Chapters Of Newly-Discovered Early Wyoming Valley History Together With Many Biographical Sketches And Much Genealogical Material by Oscar Jewell Harvey, Volume 1, page, 272, Abiel Abbott

John Tomson

Lieutenant
Served in King Philip's War Before 1643-After 1673
Of the Abbott / Cary line

John Tomson was born on the 10th of September, 1616 to John and Beatrice Detton Thompson in Wales, not Scotland as some documents suggest. He was John Tomson of Cummaquid and Patuxet, renamed Barnstable and Plymouth, Massachusetts.

Some say that John emigrated to the Colonies in the third arrival to Plymouth. The six year old John was suspected to have been on one of the two vessels under the patronage of Thomas Weston of London, arriving in May of 1622.

Image source: Massachusetts, Town Clerk, Vital and Town Records, 1626-2001, FamilySearch

Vital and town records.

Stone marking the site of the home of Lieut. John Tomson.

Image source: Chip 5610, Find-A-Grave

His chief business was that of a farmer and his first appearance in that capacity was at Sandwich. Carpenter work was probably taken up from necessity not as a trade; being a man fruitful of expedients and of uncommon ingenuity.

He was Sergeant Tomson as of the 17th of December, 1673 and was reported in August 1643, to be on the list of males of Plymouth between 16 and 60 years able to bear arms.

John had dealings on the 1st of November 1673, with the Sachem of the Neponsets in what is now the town of Middleborough, Massachusetts.

He was a Lieutenant in 1675-6 and was, by the Governor and Council, given command of the garrison and the garrison in the field. He served actively in such command during King Philip's War.

When the Dutch occupied New York and New Jersey in 1673, the Plymouth Court declared war against them and the Governor bestowed a halbert upon Sergeant Tomson.

His wife was Mary Cooke, daughter of Francis Cooke, of the "Mayflower" Company. Lt. Tomson died on the 16th of June, 1696 and is buried at Nemasket Hill Cemetery in Middleborough, Plymouth Co., Massachusetts.

Sources:

74. FamilySearch.org, Family Tree online database, https://www.familysearch.org/tree/person/details/LHJY-CGC, accessed 3 Mar 2019

75. Thompson Genealogy page 22, FamilySearch, https://www.familysearch.org/photos/artifacts/35062465?p=19988398&returnLabel=John%20Tomson%20(LHJY-CGC)&returnUrl=https%3A%2F%2Fwww.familysearch.org%2Ftree%2Fperson%2Fmemories%2FLHJY-CGC, accessed 3 Mar 2019

Memorial to John Tomson and his wife, Mary Cooke.

76. Find A Grave website, https://images.findagrave.com/photos/2018/360/16219659_8a843d22-60a8-404b-9c9d-57d9405e378f.jpeg, accessed 3 Mar 2019Find A Grave website, https://www.findagrave.com/memorial/16219659/john-tomson, accessed 3 Mar 2019

77. "Massachusetts, Town Clerk, Vital and Town Records, 1626-2001," database with images, FamilySearch (https://familysearch.org/ark:/61903/1:1:FC9Z-ML4 : 4 November 2017), Lt. John Thompson, 16 Jun 1696; citing Death, Middleborough, Plymouth, Massachusetts, United States, , town clerk offices, Massachusetts; FHL microfilm 945,016., accessed 2 Mar 2019

Shipping Off A Dutch Harbour by Gerrit Pompe, 1680

78. Ancestry, https://www.ancestry.com/mediaui-viewer/collection/1030/tree/158065724/person/402074031748/media/d59595a9-16c7-44b1-b149-702334c4ccd3?_phsrc=Sea114&usePUBJs=true, accessed 3 Mar 2019

79. Descendants of Francis Cooke, Ancestors of Captain Philip Reade, 3d Regiment of Infantry, U.S. Army : who, in a military capacity, aided to create, defend and preserve the colonies of North America between 1607 and 1776. by Philip Hildreth Reade, 1844- Fort Snelling, Minn. (1886) pg 5 / Reel/Fiche Number: Genealogy and local history ; G5266 http://starlight921.homestead.com/CookeMaryofFrancis.html?from=lynx1UIV7&treeref=LHJY-CGC,accessed 3 Mar 2019

Image Credits

Abbott, Christopher Shawn;
— Image source: IMG_0070.JPG
— Image source: IMG_0071.JPG

Abbott, Dale Cary;
— (1958) Image source: Dale Cary Abbott 1.jpg
— (1958) Image source: Dale Cary Abbott 2.jpg
— (1958) Image source: Dale Cary Abbott 3.jpg
— (1958) Image source: Dale Cary Abbott 4.jpg
— (2018) Image credit: MIDWAY L25a.jpeg
— (2018) Image credit: DSC01003 KnT 14x11.jpeg (will be the author image if chosen)
— Image source: Samuel Bennett Abbott.jpg

Abbott, Janice Louise;
— (1972) Image source: Shawn, Neal, Dale Abbott.jpg
— (2019) Image source: Headstone of Frank Wynn Bringard.jpg

Abbott, Lawrence Weston;

(1957) Image source: Lawrence Weston Abbott-3rd Class Petty Officer.jpg
— (1957) Image source: Lawrence Weston Abbott-US Navy.jpg
— (1958) Image source: LW Abbott aboard ship bef dc 2nd Cls Pty Ofcr.jpg

Abbott, Neal Alan;
— (1970) Image source: Neal Abbott.jpg

Abbott, Trula Marie Cary;

(1961) Image credit: Lawrence, Neal, Dale, friend-1961 out boot camp.jpg
— Image source: Elisha W & Flora Ann Barnaby Franklin Family.png

Adobe Stock Photos; by Ungvar, American constitution on of vintage parchment the document detail the United States Declaration of Independence with 4th july 1776, AdobeStock_360358368.jpeg

Ancestry.com Operations Inc. Lehi, UT, USA;
— (2019) Elisha W Franklin

— (2019) John Thomson
— (2019) John W Philpott
— (2019) JW Philpot
— McClure, N. J. P.; Image source: Stephen Harding Headstone.png

Bartell, Allen; Image source: EW Franklin 14th Reg Co K.jpeg

Bennett, Fred Ashby, (2001) Letter of July 12, 2001 to Dan Bringard

Bringard, Dan; Image credit: Journal Pages

Bringard, Weltha Clark;
— (1941) Image source: Earl Bringard 2.jpeg
— (1942) Image source: Gerald and Donna Philpott 1942.jpg
— (1942) Image source: Gerald Boone and Janice Louise Philpott - Feb 1944.jpg

BYU Center For Family History; Image source: Riley Garner Clark, US Mexican War Mormon Battalion.jpg

FamilySearch.org Family Tree;
— Abbott, P. D.; Image source: Abbott, James White House Certificate for his Revolutionary War Service.jpeg
— CarolynE (contributor 49714516), Image source: Stephen III Harding Revolutionary Plaque.png
— Christiansen, David Clair; Image source: Cemetery Sgt James Abbott.png
— Christiansen, David Clair; Image source: James Abbott Headstone.png
— Field, Ronda; Image source: Newspaper Article John Tomson submitted by Ronda Field FamilySearch.png
— Giberson, Lea; Image source: Frederick and Sophia.jpeg
— Giberson, Lea; Image source: Frederick William Fuhrmeister.jpeg
— Knight, William; Image source: Abiel Abbott (1724) Gravestone.jpeg
— Knight, William; Image source: Sgt James Abbott Memorial.png
— Massachusetts Society of the Sons of the American Revolution, Image source: Massachusetts Society of the Sons of the American Revolution, Register for 1904 with lists of members and their

Revolutionary an.png
— "Massachusetts, Town Clerk, Vital and Town Records, 1626-2001," Image source: Lt John Tomson Massachusetts, Town Clerk, Vital and Town Records, 1626-2001.jpg
— Middleton, Jennifer Lynn; Image source: Colonel John Franklin.jpg
— Olson, Gina Marie; Image source: Lietenant John Tomson.jpg
— Pennsylvania Cemetery Records, Image source: Stephen Harding cemetery record. jpg
— Pennsylvania Probate Records, 1683-1994; Image source: Pennsylvania Probate Records Image 105 Stephen Harding.jpg
— Strausbaugh, Caleb; Image source: Captain John William Philpot.jpeg
— Whipple, Leah; Image source: Friedrick Wilhem Christoph Fuhrmeister-Prussian Soldier.jpg

Find a Grave online database;
— Chip 5610, Image source: John Tomson Home Memorial.jpeg
— Chip 5610, Image source: Memorial to John Tomson & Mary Cooke.jpg
— Image source: Kimberly, contributor 46494736; Headstone of Samuel Bennett Abbott.jpg
— Image source: RC, Memorial ID 17470928; Alvin P Barnaby SUVCW Project.png

Mays, Kathleen Cary Abbott;
— (1992) Image credit: CNA 1992.jpg
— (2011) Image credit: Christopher Shawn Abbott.jpg
— (2011) Image credit: Christopher Shawn Abbott Back.jpg
— (2011) Image credit: CSA Grad 11x14.jpg
— (2011) Image credit: Dale Cary Abbott and Christopher Shawn Abbott.jpg
— (2018) Image credit: IMG_6152a.jpeg
— (2018) Image credit: IMG_6170.jpeg
— (2018) Image credit: IMG_6176a v2.jpeg
— (2018) Image credit: IMG_6186.jpeg
— (2018) Image credit: IMG_6291a.jpeg
— (2019) Image credit: KCMP1765.jpeg
— (2022) Image credit: Seaman, Then and Now v7.jpg
— (2023) Image credit: Dad and Kathleen collage.PNG

Minchey, Amber;
— (2000) Image credit: Earl C Bringard Headstone.png
— Image credit: Pioneer Memorial Cemetery

Earl C Bringard.png

National Archives and Records Administration;
— Image source: Earl C Bringard US Army Index.jpeg
— Image source: Gerald B Philpott, _United States World War II Army Enlistment Records, 1938-1946_ FamilySearch.org. pdf
— Image source: S Bennett Abbott, Military Service Card.jpg
— Image source: U.S., Spanish American War Volunteers Index to Compiled Military Service Records, 1898; Elisha W Franklin.jpg
— Last Action Report Of The Adjutant General, secondary image source: Neal Abbott
— U.S. Returns from Regular Army Infantry Regiments, 1821-1916; Image source: Elisha W Franklin.jpg

North Carolina State Archives; Image source: GB Philpott Military Service Discharge 1945.jpg

Peck, LaDonna Bringard
— (1965) Image credit: IMG_20190428_0001-v2.jpg
— (1965) Image source: img020.jpg

Pixabay.com; Image credit: veteran-1807121.jpg

Record, Austin James
— (2022) Image credit: Lost Sailor Setting. JPG
— (2022) Image credit: Painting USS Midway by Richard DeRosset.JPG
— (2022) Image credit: Plane on USS Midway.JPG
— (2022) Image credit: Stained Glass USS Midway.JPG
— (2022) Image credit: Anchor Chain.JPG
— (2022) Image credit: USS Midway Model. JPG
— (2022) Image credit: Gold Anchor USS Midway.JPG
— (2022) Image credit: Hanging Flag.JPG

Schmelding, Allen Bartell; Image source: Elisha W Franklin.jpg

Stalfers, Mary Jo; Image source: Riley Garner Clark.jpeg

Wikimedia Commons; <https://commons. wikimedia.org/wiki/>
— Charles D. Melson; Cartographic and visual information: George C. MacGillivray and W. Stephen Hill, Public

domain, RabaulStrategicArea.jpg

— Des Barres, Joseph F. W. (Joseph Frederick Wallet); Public domain, Chart_of_Plymouth_Bay._LOC_77693976.jpg

— Naval History & Heritage Command, Public domain, (1968) USS_Samuel_Gompers_(AD-37)_insignia,_1968_(NH_69609-KN).png

— Naval History & Heritage Command, Public domain, (1968) USS_Samuel_Gompers_(AD-37)_underway_off_the_coast_of_Oahu_on_24_November_1968_(NH_96875).jpg

— PH1 J.D. Osborne, U.S. Navy, Public domain, (1963) USS_Midway_(CV-41)_underway_1963.jpg

— Pompe, Gerrit, (1680) Shipping Off A Dutch Harbour by Gerri Pompe, Public domain, File:Shipping_Off_a_Dutch_Harbour_RMG_BHC0853.tiff

— Post-Work: W.Wolny Licence: Public Domain, Public domain, Airraid_at_Rabaul_Harbor.jpg

— US Army, Public domain, (2020) Reception_battalion_barracks,_Fort_Jackson,_SC_(2020).jpg

— US Army, Public domain, (2023) 1st_Bn_13th_Inf_crest.jpg

— U.S. Navy, Public domain, (1953) XF3H_Demon_on_USS_Coral_Sea_(CVA-43)_in_1953.jpg

— U.S. Navy, Public domain, (1955) USS_Coral_Sea_(CVA-43)_maneuvers_at_high_speed_on_28_July_1955.jpg

Bibliography

Abbott, Alexis Ann Busath; (2019) Details of the military service of Christopher Shawn Abbott

Abbott, Christopher Shawn;
— (2019) Details of the military service of Christopher Shawn Abbott

Abbott, Dale Cary;
— (2018) Interviewed by Kathleen C. Mays, 11 September 2018
— (2019) Details of the military service of Dale Cary Abbott
— (2019) Details of the military service of Samuel Bennett Abbott

Abbott, Lawrence Weston;
— (2019) Details of the military service of Lawrence Weston Abbott

Abbott, Neal Alan;
— (2019) Details of the military service of Neal Alan Abbott
— (2019) Details of the military service of Samuel Bennett Abbott

Ancestry.com Operations Inc. Lehi, UT, USA;
— (2009) "U.S., Civil War Soldier Records and Profiles, 1861-1865"
— (2011) "U.S., Confederate Soldiers Compiled Service Records, 1861-1865"
— (2011) "U.S., Returns from Regular Army Infantry Regiments, 1821-1916"
— (2012) "U.S. Spanish American War Volunteers Index to Compiled Military Service Records, 1898"
— McClure, N. J. P.; Image source: Stephen Harding Headstone.png

Bennett, Fred Ashby, (2001) Letter of July 12, 2001 to Dan Bringard

Bent, Samuel Arthur; (1904) Register for 1904 with lists of members and their Revolutionary ancestors

Blair, Williams T.; (1924) The Michael Shoemaker Book, International Press, Scranton, PA.

Boyle, Henry G.; (1847) Autobiography and Diary of Henry G. Boyle, 1832–1855

Bringard, Frank Wynn; (2019) Details of the military service of Frank Wynn Bringard

— (1960) Genealogical Records given to LaDonna Bringard Peck

Brittanica;
— (2023) "Queen Elizabeth, British Passenger Ships," Written and fact-checked by, The Editors of Encyclopaedia Britannica
— "Wyoming Massacre, United States History"

Carolana, (2023) "The American Revolution in North Carolina"

Carter, Ada Clark; (2014) "Biography of Riley Garner Clark by Ada Clark Carter"

Collegiate Water Polo Association, https://collegiatewaterpolo.org/john-t-blackburn-united-states-naval-academy-alumnus-water-polo-athlete-aviator-double-ace-founding-commander-of-the-jolly-rogers/, accessed 28 January 2023

Daughters of the American Revolution; Genealogy Research, Stephen Strawn

FamilySearch.org Family Tree;
— (2014) "United States Index to Service Records, War with Spain, 1898"
— (2014) "United States World War II Army Enlistment Records, 1938-1946"
— (2017) "Massachusetts Town Clerk, Vital and Town Records, 1626-2001"
— (2019) "35th Regiment North Carolina Infantry"
— (2019) "Discharge and Statement of Service Records, 1940-1948"
— (2019) Elisha W. Franklin, Member ID KP4M-TLD
— (2019) Frederick William Christoph Fuhrmeister, Member ID KWJC-YTX
— (2019) John Tomson, Member ID LHJY-CGC
— (2019) Thompson Genealogy
— (2020) "Pennsylvania Cemetery Records, ca. 1700-ca. 1950"
— (2020) "Utah, World War II Index to Army Veterans of Utah, 1939-1945"
— (2023) Abiel Abbott, Captain, Member ID L8ZZ-YX1
— (2023) Alvin Pope Barnaby, Member ID

LW9W-CB5
— (2023) Earl Clark Bringard, Member ID LKG1-WQ8
— (2023) Gerald Boone Philpott, Member ID LHXD-C7N
— (2023) James Abbott, Member ID L635-X92
— (2023) Wait Bradford, Member ID LZGQ-KV3
— "Michigan, County Marriages, 1820-1940," database with images, FamilySearch (https://familysearch.org/ark:/61903/3:1:939J-4K9F-YX?cc=1810350&wc=Q868-NHL%3A150747501%2C150767401 : 11 May 2018), Cass > Marriages, 1845-1858, v. B2 > image 160 of 274; various archives, Michigan.

Find a Grave online database;
— (2006) Lieut John Tomson, Memorial ID 16219659
— (2009) Capt Stephen Harding, Memorial ID 41636728
— (2009) Col John Franklin, Memorial ID 43432551
— (2011) Capt Abiel Abbott, Memorial ID 79973459
— A. P. Barnaby profile, (https://www.findagrave.com/memorial/17470928/alvin-pope-barnaby: accessed 18 April 2023), memorial page for Alvin Pope Barnaby (18 Oct 1821–13 Mar 1881), Find a Grave Memorial ID 17470928, citing North Star Cemetery, North Star, Gratiot County, Michigan, USA; Maintained by Glenn Geirland (contributor 40342511).

Foremaster, Florence (1977) Life and History of Frederick William Foremaster, 1821-1892

Global Security, Navy Ranges, Virginia Capes Operating Area VACAPES OPAREA

Harvey, Oscar Jewell, (1909) History of Wilkes-Barre, Lucerne County, Pennsylvania, From Its First Beginnings To The Present Time; Including Chapters Of Newly-Discovered Early Wyoming Valley History Together With Many Biographical Sketches And Much Genealogical Material

Hyde, William (1874) The Private Journal of William Hyde

Massachusetts, Office of the Secretary of State (1908) Massachusetts Soldiers And Sailors Of The War Of The Revolution, a compilation from the archives, Volume 2

Mays, Kathleen Cary Abbott;
— (2018) JKabbrisons Photography, The USS Midway & Navy Pride
— (2019) Personal Knowledge

Meredith, Laurie Camille Abbott (2019) Details of the military service of Lawrence Weston Abbott

Metcalf, Brandon J., (2019) Four Things to Know about the Journey of the Mormon Battalion, Church of Jesus Christ of Latter Day Saints

Midway Sailor;
— "USS Midway CV-41", https://www.midwaysailor.com/midway/history.html, accessed 14 September, 2018
— "USS Midway Commanding Officers," https://www.midwaysailor.com/midway/commandoff.html. accessed 15 September 2018

Military.com, "The Two Navy Holidays: Navy Birthday and Navy Day" https://www.military.com/navy-birthday/the-two-navy-holidays.html, accessed 13 September 2018

Military Bases website, <https://militarybases.com/overseas/germany/darmstadt/>, viewed 4 Mar 2019, accessed 4 Mar 2019

The Mormon Battalion Association (1954) "Soldiers in the Mormon Battalion, Alphabetical List of Soldiers"

National Archives and Records Administration;
— Last Action Report Of The Adjutant General, secondary image source: Neal Abbott

National Naval Naval History Aviation http://www.navalaviationmuseum.org/history-up-close/navy-day/, accessed 14 September 2018

National Park Service (2001) "The Civil War Soldiers and Sailors Database"

National Personnel Records Centers, Primary-National Personnel Records Centers, Military Personnel Records, 9700 Page Boulevard, St. Louis, Missouri 63132-5100

Naval Heritage and History, https://www.history.navy.mil/our-collections/photography/us-navy-ships/aircraft-carriers.htm,l accessed 28 January 2023

NavSource Naval History, "NavSource Online: Aircraft Carrier Photo Archive," http://www.navsource.org/archives/02/41.htm, accessed 27 January 2023

Navy: "Together We Served, No Stronger Bond, USS Samuel Gompers (AD 37) Tender / Repair Ship"

Peck, LaDonna Bringard
— (1987) Personal Knowledge

Reade, Philip Hildreth (1886) Descendants of Francis Cooke, Ancestors of Captain Philip Reade, 3d Regiment of Infantry, U.S. Army: who, in a military capacity, aided to create, defend and preserve the colonies of North America between 1607 and 1776.

Revolutionary War dot US (2017) "Connecticut Regiments in the Continental Army"

Thomas Legion (2005) "35th North Carolina Infantry Regiment: Battles and Casualties"

United States Public Health Service (2019) Federal Security Agency, United States Public Health Service, National Office of Vital Statistics

Utah State Archives and Records Service Salt Lake City, Utah (1975) "Military Service Cards, ca. 1898-1975"

Wikipedia, The Free Encyclopedia
— (2013) "Mormon Battalion"
— (2018) "USS Midway", https://en.m.wikipedia.org/wiki/USS_Midway_(CV-41), accessed 12 September 2018
— (2019) "Battle of Wyoming"
— (2019) "National Personnel Records Center fire"
— (2023) "Battle of Midway", https://en.m.wikipedia.org/wiki/Battle_of_Midway, accessed 27 January 2023

About the Author:

Born in Delta, a small rural community in west-central Utah, Kathleen was raised in the Salt Lake valley from age two. Her enthusiasm toward animals, particularly canines, felines, and equines, developed at a very young age. Throughout her childhood years, she acquired other interests in genealogy, photography, sketching, and nature.

Her parents, Dale and Louise, always made it a high priority of creating memories for their two daughters through family events. Camping, motorcycling, organized sports, music, and exploring God's amazing world throughout North America were some of their chosen activities. They learned very young, after the tragic loss of two of their four children, to make the best of their time as a family.

Our author is currently living in Utah's Salt Lake Valley with her husband, her Miniature Australian Shepherd, her three cats, her turtle, and her two parakeets. She adores her three grown sons and considers motherhood to be owner of her most cherished blessings.

Kathleen has been passionate about family history since childhood. She has collected stories and information to add to her personal collection for decades.

Kathleen and Her Sister, Teresa, 2018.

Some of her most cherished memories are of her time listening and learning about family traditions and ancestral details.

"I've been asked why I love family history so much. I think about that question and several reasons come to mind. One interesting factor is my love of learning about genetics and familial health issues. I cannot deny the positive impact of knowing I belong. Genealogy personalizes history, with the ancestral stories. Most importantly, it fills me up." KCM

About the Designer:

Austin James Record was born and raised in Salt Lake City, Utah. He grew up with an enthusiastic interest in art, photography, music, LEGO®, bonsai, and video games. Throughout the years his family has had many animals but he prefers caring for cats.

He studied graphic design at Salt Lake Community College and completed his bachelor's degree at the University of Utah. His creative passion started at a very young age that was cultivated by supportive family members.

Austin has become a skilled graphic designer through the experience of working on projects for various output mediums. His perspective of each project transforms the details in pieces of a puzzle to achieve the desired outcome. His favorite types of projects involve the complexity of signage, large format printing, and anything involved with establishing and optimizing a brand.

At this time, Austin lives with his partner, their Jack Russell Terrier and their four cats. Together they manage vacation rental properties and vehicles.

Austin and His Mother, Kathleen, 2013.

If you would like to order this book, you can do so through the publisher's website.

www.JRemington press.com

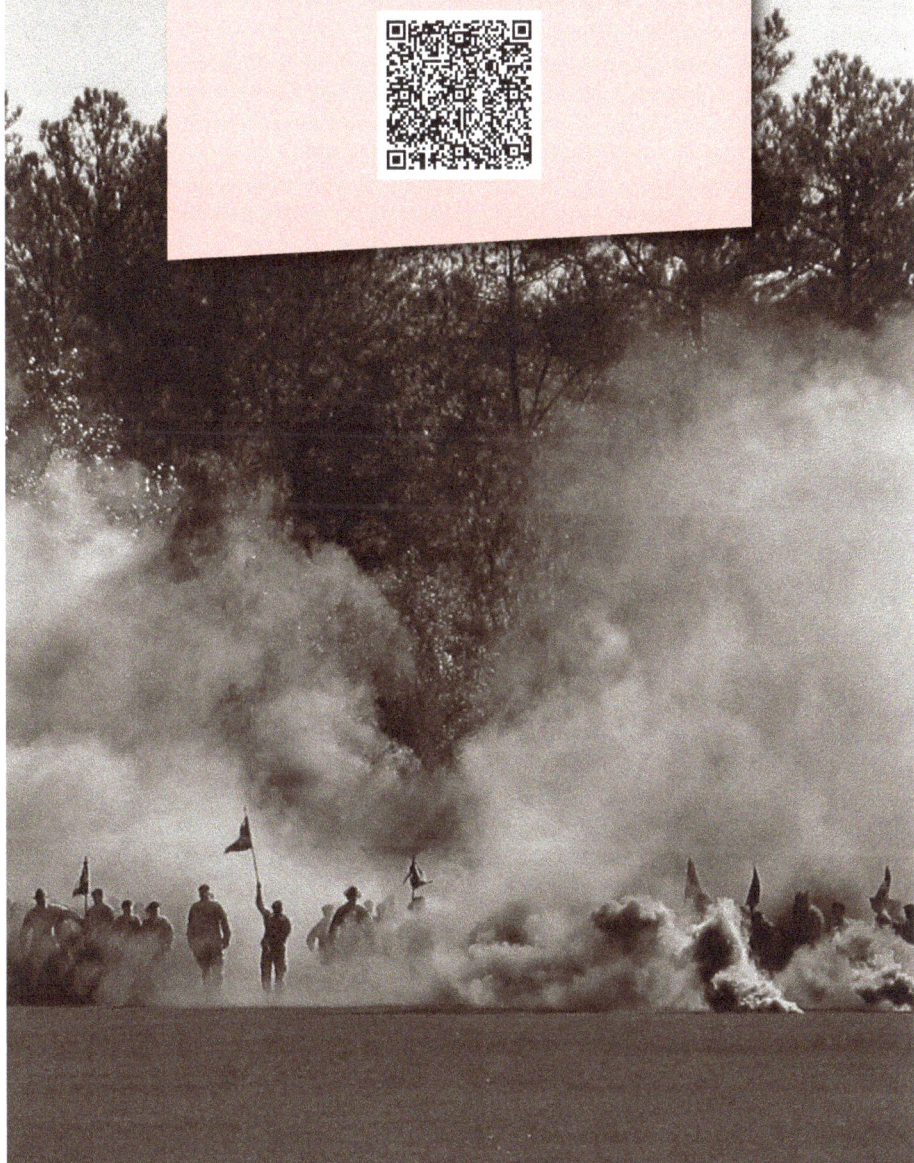

www.ingramcontent.com/pod-product-compliance
Lightning Source LLC
Chambersburg PA
CBHW041930260326
41914CB00009B/1242